MISFITS & MINISTRY

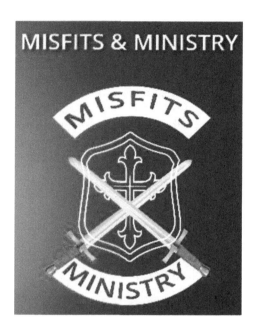

15 STORIES OF LIFE TRANSFORMATION FROM MISFITS NOW DOING MINISTRY

CHAPLAIN GERALD K. POTOKA

DISCLAIMER

The conversations within this book are all of the author's recollections, though they are not written to represent word for word transcripts. These are the collections of the author's personal stories, from each of their perspectives. All events are represented as faithfully as possible.

No part of this book may be reproduced or used in any manner without the prior written permission of the copyright owner, except for the use of brief quotations in a book review. Request for permission to reproduce selections from this book should be emailed to the author: gpotoka52@gmail.com.

Cover design: Young's Solutions LLC
                       www.youngssolutionsllc.com

Edited by: J.D. Johnson

Paperback ISBN: 9798373853767
Copyright © 2023 Chaplain Gerald Potoka

Published by: Young's Solutions LLC.,
                       Columbia, SC 29210
                       www.youngssolutionsllc.com

TABLE OF CONTENTS

FOREWORD

This collection of testimony is a practical example of how God continues to work in the lives of those that choose to accept, believe, and receive Him through His son Jesus Christ. Although the authors' backgrounds differ subtly in some places and vastly in others, the fact that we are all broken and in need of a savior permeates throughout mankind's history – and so it goes within this book.

I was asked to write my story early on during this project but decided not to for personal reasons. However, it has been my absolute pleasure reading, editing, and remaining involved until its completion. Some of the authors I know personally and have worked closely alongside for many years (and still maintain working relationships with some of them). Then there are those I haven't had the opportunity to get acquainted with, but by their riveting testimonies have developed an empathetic connection.

When the first book "***Misfits & Miracles***" was written, the author stepped out on faith and set a precedent for other misfits by speaking candidly about man's sinful nature before Christ and then boldly declaring God's saving grace and unmerited favor for all who would dare to seek Him for themselves.

"***Misfits & Ministry***" helps to demystify God's presence and power in the lives of seemingly average yet extraordinarily diverse individuals. God is not to be placed inside a box or be concluded upon by our simpleminded, finite wisdom. As you read each story, experience how God transforms lives according to His will and good pleasure. See also how each author willingly submits their lives to God's ultimate authority and how He turns tragedy into triumph – and misfits into ministry!

J.D. Johnson
Clerk, Editor, Arrangement

INTRODUCTION

After my first book, *"Misfits & Miracles"* was published, several readers contacted me and told me that they were misfits too, and I

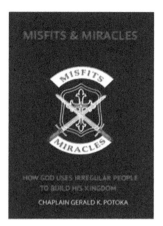

needed to hear their story. So, I asked them to write it down to be included in this second Misfits book; and I also asked other friends for their stories as well. Everyone loves a story with a happy ending, especially when you can see the hand of God at work bringing healing and wholeness. As you will see, most of the following stories are prison related – after all, I am a prison chaplain. Other stories are not prison-related, but from personal friends with a history of poor life choices, addictions, abuse, or personal struggles that qualify them as misfits who have been transformed by the grace of God. I asked each writer to follow a general outline that gave some hints of how their lives got off track: The family in which you grew up – religious, normal, dysfunctional, abusive, etc.

- Decisions you made early in life that were good or bad for you.
- How and when things went wrong and what consequences you experienced.
- How and when God began to draw you to Himself and who He used in that process.
- How you came to surrender your life to Christ.
- How God is using you now to influence people's lives and minister to their needs.

My prayer for those reading this book is that you would be comforted and encouraged, challenged, and motivated to transition your life from a misfit to one who ministers to the people around you that need to hear about God's rescue plan of redemption and to serve God by loving others as you love yourself.

Chap

"Therefore, if anyone is in Christ, he is a new creation; old things have passed away; behold, all things have become new" (2 Corinthians 5:17 NKJV).

RUSTY

Born in the 1950s and adopted at the age of three, I grew up in Bunnell, Florida where my dad's family was well-established. Dad was raised to be a rancher and he was a very well-known and respected member of the community. But soon after adoption, I suffered the most impactful loss of my life - the day of my father's death.

 My mother, now newly widowed, could not continue managing a large ranch as well as be a single parent with three small children. So, she moved us to a small South Florida town, named Vero Beach. She struggled to be a single mother, nurturing caregiver, and sole provider.

I grew up quickly and learned instinctively how to be discontent, envious, and aggressive. I felt I was different from other kids who had both a mother and father. I hated not having a dad like my friends and other kids around me. My whole world was one of dreaming about being in a close family. Now I could never see myself as being like the other kids. It took a horrible wound like fatherlessness, to make me feel like I would never be able to be loving and accepting of myself. This one single event, the death, and absence of my father set the course for a childhood of extreme anger, bitterness, and resentment, and established the direction of my life – toward poor choices, bad behaviors, and a bad attitude. That came to define me as a malcontent.

From then on, failure would be accompanied by rebellion, anger, and almost always non-compliant with socially acceptable behavior. I reveled in my loneliness and was acting out continually. I resented being given up for adoption, then resented being abandoned by the dad I was given to, by his untimely death. Anger didn't just control me - it defined who I was, and I fed on it every day of my life. I loved my mother very much. She was a working single mother who provided everything I needed, except time. She did her best to provide the necessary elements for growing children, but I never could get her to take time off and just be a mother for us – we missed out on quality living. She had grown up extremely poor and hungry and she became fiercely committed to never letting her children go without food, proper clothing, or a roof over their heads.

My downward slide, my rite of passage as a misfit, began when I was about 13 years old. Drugs and alcohol became my constant companions. Lacking the presence of proper parental supervision, I continued to descend into a constant state of mind-altering substance abuse. I disregarded any moral or ethical limits or considerations as a part of my lifestyle. Physical correction by my mother, and sometimes school authorities, did not work. Military school did not have any effect on me either. I ran away from home several times and eventually ended up in New York City, where I lived a bohemian lifestyle of self-indulgence and reckless, dangerous living. When I did finally return home, I officially dropped out of school and joined the United States Marine Corps. But that didn't end well either.

Due to my uncontrolled anger, unrestrained alcohol and drug usage, and negative racial beliefs, I was granted an early release from the Marine Corps, somehow under *honorable* conditions. Not long after leaving the military, I coerced (kidnapped) a young girl from Ft. Myers, Florida, and sold her on the streets of New York City. While on the run from the authorities in both Florida and New York, I ended up moving to Charleston, SC, where I found refuge in the company of a motorcycle gang named the Tribulators (now the Hell's

Angels of South Carolina.) This biker lifestyle led me to adopt the mindset that I was invincible, and that I had the authority and power to impose my will on any person. My appetites and my desires were my rules – no one was exempt

from my imposition of the superiority of Panhandler (aka Rusty.) It did not take long for me to achieve the humorous prestige of getting every member of the Tribulators legally barred and banned, by court order, from the premises of all 7-Eleven convenience stores in South Carolina. We were to be detained and arrested upon violation of any part of the court order. But I thought they were my personal suppliers of all tobacco and alcohol products that I may ever want or need at any time of the day or night. I felt like the operator of any 7-Eleven was my personal assistant. My form of currency for all supplies was intimidation – a simple verbal notification in a loud and menacing voice that said, "my name is Panhandler, I am a (blanking) Tribulator, and I can do any (blanking) thing I want to do!"

Shortly after attaining this achievement, I attended a mandatory meeting conducted at another motorcycle club's clubhouse late one night. It was a nightmare of a meeting; one for which I am still reaping the consequences. Nothing good ever came from a motorcycle gang war. In 1971 I was convicted of two counts of murder and a long litany of other crimes that resulted from this battle with the opposing motorcycle club. Here I was only 20 years old, and I was sentenced to death by electrocution by the South Carolina Department of Corrections.

 I remained on Death Row for six years until the United States Supreme Court overturned the death penalty in America, and I was re-sentenced to life in prison. I am not adequately able to describe what it is like to live on Death Row. Executions are not carried out for many years, due to appeals and courtroom maneuvers by defense lawyers, but there is a heavy weight that hangs over each man every day, every month, every year – death is coming for sure, but no one ever knows when. I am not looking for pity; I deserve everything I got. But I don't know how to make it understandable to those who have no point of reference for relatability. Life on the inside of a prison is inconceivable for those who have not experienced it. Death Row is even worse. It is a place of desperation, loneliness, and emptiness - a mere existence where the word *void* becomes understandable. It is a place where I could experience death long before my execution date arrived. But only

until I discovered my purpose for living – a transformation of life through Jesus Christ.

On Christmas day, 1977, while on lock-up for an investigation of an assault & battery on another inmate, I asked a library clerk for something to read to get my mind off the dread of spending another Christmas in prison, away from my family and hidden away from society. Certain times in prison are more difficult than others, and I especially missed my family at Christmas. The clerk returned a short time later and placed a book between the bars of my cell and kept on walking. Later that evening I retrieved the book from my cell bars and read the cover of the book titled, "*The Late Great Planet Earth*" by Hal Lindsey. I had no idea it was a religious book . . . surely not what I was looking for! When I read the back cover, it referenced a verse from the Bible found in the book of Revelation that actually said that during the Tribulation, the blood of man would run upon the face of the earth as high as the bridle of a horse. This got my attention - spilling the blood of man upon the face of the earth.

In the early morning hours as I read, I would be visited by an apparition of the Lord Himself. He began ministering life to me - altering my very being in such an impactful way as to change me and reset the trajectory of my life. My filth, my sinfulness, and my wickedness were so obvious and convicting to me at that time, in contrast to His holiness and perfection, I was literally scared to death! Terrified! I knew that I had come face-to-face with the Man above all men. The Lord Jesus Christ drew me into His marvelous light and through the help of a Christian inmate I knew in that building named Richard Valenti, I was ushered into the Kingdom of Almighty God: forgiven, cleansed, and purified through His blood, to forever be with Him.

The undeniable change that I had undergone in those brief few minutes in the presence of Jesus Christ so radically changed my life, and that became recognizable to other inmates and the administration of the Department of Corrections. Jesse W. Strickland, former warden at Central Correctional Institution (CCI) when I was on Death Row had now become the Deputy Director of the Department of Corrections. My case was reviewed by the classification board and my life change was obvious to them as well – they had reports of the changes in my behavior and attitude, as well as the undeniable presence of Christ in me. Soon I was transferred from CCI to Kirkland, another maximum custody prison, but with greater opportunities for those who had changed their lives. The Lord, along with my advocate and friend Jesse Strickland, had me reviewed by Kirkland's classification board not long after my arrival, and I was elevated to level "A" Trustee status. I was soon transferred to Lexington Correctional Institution and was permitted to work at the Department of Corrections Headquarters in their print shop. God's favor and grace were all over my life, and I was living under the direction and grace of Jesus, my King!

I continued to find favor in everything I did and all that I stood for. At Lexington, I was elevated to "AA" Trustee status. Jesse Strickland put me on the back of a fruit truck one day and had me transferred to Piedmont Work Release Center in Spartanburg. There I was given a brand-new business location to work at in Spartanburg called Taylor Rental Center. I was given my own personal company vehicle, working all day, and returning to the Institution every evening. I was given the freedom of eating dinner every night with my wife and children, tucking them into their beds, saying our prayers, and kissing them before returning to the Institution to sleep. Before I left for work again the next morning, I had time to go by and drive my children to school. Prison is tough, but God our Father is in control. I was truly living the scriptures that taught, "with God, all things are possible." I was never in a prison that was successful in keeping God out.

In 1981 I was granted Parole. Released to do ministry on the streets that I had once terrorized. I went full bore kingdom warrior for

Jesus, trying to atone for my horrible past. But I also needed to make some money to live on, so I started a business, and then another one, and soon I was more about the businesses than the ministry. I began to lose my focus and lose my way. I soon lost my marriage. Then a failed business, and another failed marriage. Within a few years, I was spinning out of control. I was again living in defiance against the God who had so dramatically rescued me – from spiritual destruction, from Death Row, and eventually from prison altogether. Now living like a lost prodigal, I tried to settle a domestic situation with gun violence, and in 2002 my Parole was revoked, and I was returned to prison to complete my life sentence.

Twenty years after having my Parole revoked and my return to prison, I am back trying to live out my life in a manner that is consistent with the will and word of God. His calling is still on my life and now I live in obedience instead of defiance. My daily prayer is that the sweet aroma of Christ in me as His obedient servant might somehow draw others into a relationship with Him. Today, although I am still incarcerated and living out my existence in a man-made prison, I am as free as any man I know. **I am free indeed!**

God continues to bless me by using me to minister and mentor many incarcerated men. I live and minister at a medium custody prison and work as a ministry assistant in the chapel. I serve all inmates in the pursuit of their faith journey and seek to point them to Christ as the only one capable of rescuing them from eternal death and separation from God. I am the primary clerk for JumpStart Ministry, Proverbs226 Ministry, Kairos Prison Ministry, and leader of the Misfits discipleship class. I am always ready and willing to be a faithful witness and testify to anyone at any time about what Christ can do for those who will surrender to His Lordship and His Sovereignty over their life, even for those of us who have failed Him miserably – we are being transformed now and will be for all Eternity!

I recently turned 72 years old, and I don't know what my earthly future looks like. I may never step foot outside of the penitentiary before God calls me home, but right now I know I am exactly where He wants me and I'm doing what He has called me to do. By the time you read this story, I will be in training for more ministry in the Columbia International University: Prison Initiative Program at another institution. I belong to Him, and He sustains me, strengthens me, and encourages me as I serve Him, the God of all creation. He has made all things new in my life.

"God treated Jesus like He had lived Rusty's sinful life, so that He could now treat Rusty like He had lived Jesus' perfect life." (2 Corinthians 5:21 The Rusty Version).

I grew up in Charlotte, North Carolina. Mom, Dad, my brother Eugene, and I lived in a two-bedroom apartment in a neighborhood known as Brookhill. I also had two stepbrothers and a stepsister  who I considered family as well. In my childlike understanding, I always considered myself well taken care of, especially not knowing anything else to compare it with; I knew of no other family dynamics to base this belief upon. Everyone in the neighborhood knew each other, and since there were no obvious 'rich folk' standouts, it felt like we were all just one big family. We seemed to be interrelated, if not by name or blood, at least by our shared experiences - sometimes a love/hate relationship. I never experienced any physical abuse as a child, but as I grew older, the mental and emotional factors began to come into play. Isn't it great to live in the shell of protection known as childhood?

Once I started to peer around closed doors and began to enter the domain of adulthood, I began to see Mom and Dad in a different light, with a new understanding of who my parents were in their private world away from the children. Dysfunction began to take on a whole new meaning. I guess once my eyes were opened, sort of like Eve in the Bible, it was a whole new and complicated world.

Mom and Dad both worked full-time jobs for as long as I remember. My life consisted of going to school, a quick stop at home before playing outside until the streetlights came on at night, having dinner, and going to bed. My Dad liked to party on the weekends. He would let us hang out for a while and see all their friends, but when the party cranked up, the liquor came out and the party began to get serious, we would be sent off to bed. This is where I discovered the curious side of my nature. I could never just go straight to bed. I began to creep and explore, and soon my eyes were opened to a lot of adult activities and grown-up behaviors.

As I got older and bolder, I began to sneak around in my parents' room when I was home alone. Imagine my surprise discovering guns, drugs, and sexually explicit materials in my parents' private space. Boy, oh boy, this thing called life, took on a whole new dimension. My dad began to come home later and later, long after Mom came in. I didn't feel safe at home until after he arrived home, considering the neighborhood we lived in. Because of all the shootings and other loud noises, we would hear at night in the neighborhood, my mom, brother, and I would often hide under the bed until Dad finally came home. During the day we would hang around outside, but during the dark hours, we would all hide under the bed scared for our own lives.

As I got older, I started noticing how my dad began to change. He was drinking more, and the arguments between him and Mom were getting increasingly louder and more frequent. Dad became much more volatile, aggressive, and threatening to both us kids as well as Mom. His explosive fits of anger and violence were escalating way

 beyond what is acceptable to anyone, but especially within a family. Witnessing him continually threatening to kill my mom, brother, and me, became my teenage reality. Mom often stayed with her sisters to avoid my dad's rage and violent outbursts. Quite frequently, Eugene and I could hear Dad loading his guns at night and pacing around the house talking to himself, threatening to kill Mom if she came back home. To protect myself, I began to sleep with a gun in my bed at night, thinking I may have to kill him if, or when, he killed Mom. One night my dad and I had a falling out in the hallway between our bedrooms, and we stood face to face, with me looking down the barrel of his gun! It was the worst feeling I had ever experienced as a teenager! Dad? His gun in my face! It didn't even seem real. However, it was as real as his gun and my fear. This started my time of isolation. I distanced myself

from my family, both physically and emotionally. I was staying gone from the house for greater lengths of time. I knew they were there, but not in the way I wanted, or needed them. We were not talking anymore or interacting as a family. Just existing.

 The first time I ever sold crack, I made $100. From there forward, I was an open cannon waiting to fire. In the circle I was now running, drugs were always readily available. I did not have to seek them out - they came looking for me. I went from selling crack, to guns, and any other illegal activity that could afford me the lifestyle I was looking for. I became the baddest, toughest little 14-year-old kid in the neighborhood. My attitude was vicious, just like I learned from my dad!

By the time I turned 17, I was in jail facing 30 years in prison, with charges of armed robbery, attempted murder, kidnapping, and multiple assaults with a weapon. Downhill was my destiny, or so it would seem to an outside observer. I was seriously committed to this lifestyle that I was pursuing - I put it all out there on the streets for my people and our chosen alliance. I was willing to give it all for my people, but that was not everyone else's mindset. One of these supposed friends decided to sell me out and turned informer on me. Seventeen years old, facing a 30-year prison sentence, and I still had that ride-or-die attitude. Since this was my first time in jail, and considering my age, I was allowed to plead out to seven years in prison. But God! He spared my life. I begin to pray and seek Him while I was at the beginning of my seven-year stint. He did give me another chance…several actually!

There was this pastor that use to come into the prison twice a week for Bible study, and in order to get out of my cell for a couple of hours, I would sit through his Bible study. It didn't take long for me to begin looking forward to Pastor Dana Bryant's arrival every Tuesday and Thursday. There was just "this thing" about him that attracted me to him, and we became really close to each other. I knew that he was real and genuine and that he cared about me, so we became very attached. When I finally did get out of prison, I reached out to him, and we begin hanging out quite a bit. When he came to see me, our friendship became more real and stronger for

me. I had never known a friendship like this before. He would pick me up from work and we would have Bible study, eat together, and then he would take me back home. My parents were still heavily steeped in their dysfunction. Whenever the pastor would come to my parent's house to get me, he would hear the gunshots around the neighborhood. He thought that it was too dangerous for me to continue in that environment, so I was eventually invited to move in with him and his family. They gave me a safe place to lay my head and a peace that was so absent in my own family. I started attending his church and eventually, they helped me find my own apartment. While I was attending his church, I got involved in helping set up or serving in any capacity that they asked of me.

It was at this church that I first met another pastor, Chaplain Gerry Potoka, and quickly bonded with him. He would pick me and other misfits up in his van and off we would go to try and show others how to find the way from death to life. Eventually, I began attending church with him (in a prison) called Kershaw Correctional Institution. I never thought I would ever be going back to prison (willingly). Now my message to others was completely different. We started attending Sunday services there and having life skills classes throughout the week. During this time, I was being discipled by these men and I was observing how they were living out their lives and their treatment of other people. They were good role models for me

in so many ways. These men became the model for life that my dad could never, or would ever, fill for me. I had found a new direction that would carry me through the rest of my life, thanks to these men.

I believe my relationship with Christ had grown stronger while I was in prison. God had gotten me out of much more than a severe 30-year prison sentence. His merciful sentence of seven years allowed me to be in a place with time and opportunity to pray, read my Bible, and spend time with Him, thus allowing me to be changed and made anew!! Over time my relationship with God grew stronger; not perfect, but a whole lot stronger. I knew that I did not want to spend the rest of my life running in that same old lifestyle and continue getting the negative consequences that I had always gotten all my life. I wanted something different, something new. I wanted and desired to have a loving and close relationship with God my Father. All the people I use to run with ended up dead or in prison for life, or rather they call it life!

Since I have been home from incarceration, so many blessings and opportunities have flooded my life. I went from working a job to having a career; from sitting in a prison cell to getting my private pilot license - learning how to fly planes in order to expand my usefulness in serving God. God really does use the broken and the misfits of this world to show forth His love, mercy, power, and abilities. I am always surprised how He keeps using me in so many varied and useful ways to help grow those who are around me. One opportunity that God surprised me with has been through a program that my friend and partner, Lori, and I have named, "Project Exodus." We are removing tattoos from the faces and other obvious areas that people like myself, who have come out of a lifestyle where we proudly displayed our tattoos of gang affiliation or some other twisted and obscene living mode, in which we formerly lived. This enables those of us who have those regrettable markings on our bodies to display a new image as we attempt to live life outside of our youthful ignorance. Lori is the owner of the establishment from which we remove the obvious effects of these adverse decisions and poor choices we made early on in our world of darkness. For anyone willing to try and make some positive changes, not only in their appearance but in their decisions and actions, we will remove these tattoos from them for free. These are guys and girls who are defined in our society by their poor and ignorant choices of being affiliated with deadly gangs, white supremacy mobs, or any other antisocial representation.

I never envisioned myself removing tattoos from myself or others who were ready to leave that behind them and go on to living a new life. Project Exodus has become a well-respected and recognized ministry within our community, supporting those whom the world calls misfits, but who are positively ready to step out and begin again. Now, I see that God does have a new purpose for me in Him. As Christ went about doing good, I can be a follower of Him. Recently God has opened the door for another opportunity for ministry in my community. I was invited to be a Board Member, Mentor, and Mentorship Advisor of, *Our Daily Bread Foundation*, working to move disenfranchised people from welfare to well-fare. I am a misfit, but I am also a miracle!

God is in heaven: that is all I knew growing up. The only time I ever went to church was sometimes when I'd visit my paternal grandparents or when I'd stay the night with a friend who did go to church regularly. When I did go to church, I never paid any attention - it was boring to me since I had no clue what was being talked about. Over the years, I'd see random things at my grandma's with the name Jesus on them and I learned that Jesus was God. I was just so confused about it all; I didn't understand, and I didn't try to understand.

My parents were not churchgoers. My dad grew up Baptist and had to be in church whenever the church doors were opened, but I chose not to go as an adult. My mom is a German Catholic and she always said the Catholic Churches are not the same in the States. My dad was a truck driver and wasn't home much, and my mom stayed at home with my brother, sister, and me. Dad provided for us financially but because of his job, he wasn't always there physically and hardly ever emotionally. My mom was home all the time, and she did the best she could for us in every way possible, but it wasn't all roses. I butted heads with her a lot. Ever since I could remember I was always an angry child, and I would lash out at her verbally and attack my brother physically. In retrospect, I believe I felt misunderstood. I had a speech impediment, and I didn't know how to express my emotions, which led to anger.

I always wanted my way and I learned quickly how to get it. I would lie and manipulate, gossip, throw fits, and be absolutely hateful until I got what I wanted. It worked, so I kept doing it. I was an average student in school, but there was potential if I made an effort. As long as I passed the grade, there was no point in my mind in putting in the extra work - plus it wasn't cool to be smart and get good grades. Early in high school, I changed cliques. I thought the people who partied and smoked weed were cool, and I wanted to be friends with them, so I got my way by people-pleasing them. When the guy I had a crush on told me it would be funny if I got high, it wasn't long before I started smoking weed. Alcohol came along next and then coke and pills. There was also a phase with ecstasy, and then came heroin - my new love.

I didn't know anything about addiction or withdrawals or any other consequences of using heroin. I know I heard people had talked about all of that in the past, but I didn't pay attention – I never planned on becoming an addict. It didn't take long before I'd know exactly what addiction, withdrawal, and the negative consequences of heroin addiction would look like. I knew it well for the next nine years on and off - mostly on.

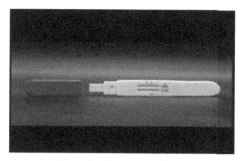

After two years of using heroin, I did stop for a couple of months and then I got pregnant. At that time, I was working with a woman who talked to me a lot about Jesus and how He rescued her. I went to church with her, and I heard every word the pastor was saying. At the end of the service when he did the altar call, I raised my hand, stood up, walked to the front of the church, and said a prayer. I was sent to a back room where they gave me a Bible, and then I left. That was it! In my mind, I was now saved, and I was going to heaven. That woman continued to talk with me about everything, and she may have told me things that I didn't pay attention to. I'm not sure. I do know it didn't change my life. Not long after that, I used again for a short time even though I was still pregnant. And then I quit using again; that's the life of an addict. I continued going to church and delivered a healthy big, beautiful baby boy on Christmas Day.

When he was about seven months old, I started using heroin again, but soon was introduced to bath salts, and the rapid downward spiral took over. My mom took my son for a short time while my dad helped me straighten up, but then I got a fresh start right back into drugs. I also started a romantic relationship with a female. She did drugs as well and we got into every drug that we possibly could. My mom came and took my son again, but it wasn't a short time this go round. You would think I'd want to get myself together for my son, but the opposite happened. My mom just took my only responsibility from me, and I went all out of control. I was soon homeless, addicted, and completely lost. I knew this wasn't the life I wanted for me, but I was not willing to change anything about it. Somehow, I had become very comfortable in this sin-filled life.

One day after a successful drug run, I got back to the motel I was staying in at the time, and I laid on the bed and I prayed. I don't know what was different about this day, but I told God that I didn't want to do drugs anymore, but I could not stop by myself. And then I forgot about it and went on doing what I always did, but this time God intervened. Not the way I wanted at all, because I went to jail. Being homeless and on drugs, I got caught stealing from Wal-Mart and sentenced to probation. Then I violated that probation; I only stayed in jail for one month and then I moved out of state and lived with my dad. He helped me get back on my feet and I soon crossed paths with someone in my family who was going to Narcotics Anonymous, so, I joined her. I was able to get clean and sober and was attending meetings regularly. I worked the 12 steps - a couple of times.

I met a fellow addict at these meetings who eventually became my sponsor. She is the one who took me through the steps the second time, and she showed me what true friendship should be; most importantly, she told me about the love of Jesus Christ. Starsha took the time to help me understand the love and freedom that Christ offered to me. I paid attention to her. I don't know why I suddenly had ears to hear but I'm forever thankful that God put her in my life. I realized I had some of the same behavioral patterns as I did when I was using drugs. Now instead of using drugs, I would use guys for approval. With a father that was emotionally unavailable during my formative years, I was looking for affirmation and acceptance from any man showing me

attention. I felt that I had to be validated by a man and I did whatever I had to do to get that. I was miserable. I didn't understand how I could not be on drugs and still be so lost. My wonderful friend painted the picture for me - I needed Christ!

I prayed and surrendered my life to Christ, and I meant every word of it. Starsha did what she was called to do. Jesus had delivered her from a very similar lifestyle, so she held my hand along this journey. She read the Bible with me, taught me, guided me, and prayed for me and with me. I got into the Word of God, and I was being convicted of a whole lot more sin than I ever realized was possible. It hurt, but it

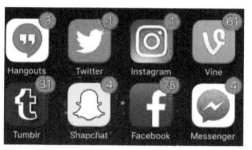 was a good hurt. I had never been so hungry for something. I removed all distractions from my life. I deleted all my social media, and I read and studied the Word of God consistently. I started going to a good church, tried to get involved in the church as much as I could, and developed positive and encouraging relationships with other Christians. Everything I have ever craved in my life I found fulfilled in Jesus Christ. He is my forever true love. Getting to know God has been the most satisfying endeavor of my life - I am in complete awe of His love for me.

After a few years of taking it all in for myself, I realized I needed to get out there and tell everyone else the good news! But not many people I have come across have wanted to hear what I have to say. It's heartbreaking and discouraging. I prayed about it and did what Matthew 5:16 says, "Let your light shine before men in such a way that they may see your good works and glorify your Father who is in heaven."

My son, almost a teenager now, started asking me questions about Jesus and sin. Sometimes it was like talking to a wall, but God soon opened his heart and my son received Jesus into his life. I am so thankful that the Lord saved me and loves me like He does. I get to take my son to church, I get to minister to him, I get to teach him about Jesus and go through the Word with him - and I get to be his mom. Since he has been saved, he has had friends asking him questions about God and it has been an amazing thing to watch. I have some friends I made in the NA meetings, and I sometimes get to share my story of rescue and redemption with them. One of them was going through a very bad relapse, and I stayed in touch with him because I wanted him to know that God loves him, and so did I. He got clean, thank God, and he surrendered his life to Christ!

My whole life I did what I wanted to do; whatever made me feel good. The result was that I didn't feel good at all, and I was hopelessly lost. Psalm 37:4 says, "Delight yourself in the Lord; And He will give you the desires of your heart." That's what I did and that's what He did. I am a Misfit, but I am also a Miracle!

BRUCE

I was born in New Britain, Connecticut, to a very unstable family. My father, whom I never had a chance to know, left my mom when I was three months old. I was told he was an abusive alcoholic. We were

raised Roman Catholic, worshipping who I perceived to be a very punishing God. Although I was raised half-heartedly in the church by the strict rules of Catholicism, it was far different from what went on behind closed doors. There were insults, fights, and aggression at the center of all the conversations in our family - secrets were kept tighter than confession on Sundays with the priest. God was certainly not the leading topic in our broken house: arguments and fighting were, and that increased as the holidays approached. Holidays were just dress rehearsals for what our family wasn't in real life. No dad, welfare, free school lunches, food stamps, and moving to one apartment after another were many of the embarrassments I would face. It was all the dysfunction a child could swallow in a lifetime.

I was a loner, a recluse of sorts. I always felt alone and different from my siblings, and very detached from the entire family; there was never a sense of bonding among us. My oldest sister whom I loved very much, was wild and out of control. I remember her getting kicked out of Jr. High School because she threatened the principal and threw something at him. My brother was very protective of me but very angry and I bore the brunt of his emotions when he was drunk or high. We lived in the same bedroom until he left to live with our father, so we stopped talking to each other for the next 20 years. Then I received a phone call that he was dead. I knew he was an addict because I am the one who turned him on to crack early in my own addiction. My family shunned me for that, even denying that his death was related to drugs.

All these secrets were kept behind closed doors. That is where I learned to hide the truths of my own sorrows, regrets, and unresolved pain. No one would have believed me if I told them what went on in our family. I learned to hate my family - especially my mom. I blamed her for me not having a dad. I blamed her for this force-fed poison of religion. All I knew is that we were Catholics, and I didn't want anything to do with that. My best friend and I were supposed to go to mass on Sundays and report back to Mom what was taught. Of course, we would only attend for a moment in case mom had spies watching us, then we would leave. We were more interested in playing nerf football. I could never figure out how Mom knew that I didn't really attend. Spies? No! Much later I realized Mom went to a Mass of Replication of Sunday's mass. I was busted and sent to catechism classes at Our Lady of Mercy School with mean Sister Mary. No mercy for me from Sister Mary – her corporal punishment gave me more reason to hate the God thing.

It wasn't long before I finally overtly rebelled. I didn't start out using drugs, but my bad behavior led me to my first drug use early in life and a short pathway to hell's fury. Our Sunday church farce looked like Utopia on the outside, but I knew that hell waited for me around the corner. And sure enough, on Monday we would return to family hell. What kind of God would leave me alone in such pain, without a father and no connection to anyone positive – I was an outcast in my own family. I was too young to deal with this hatred brewing inside of me; the more I heard about God the more I hated him. I didn't choose this kind of life, so I rejected everything about it. How does a child grow up so lost and cold and become a regular menace to society?

Addiction doesn't ask your permission to ruin you, and it often never first comes in the form of an illegal substance. My first addiction was pure hatred and the adrenalin that caused me to draw a line in the sand against good morals, values, and behaviors. My moral dividing line was erased at

a very early age. Active addiction would eventually remove that moral compass altogether, and I became spiritually bankrupt and soon adapted to suffering, longing to have just one more fix, one more high to get through the day. The first event that led to my demise occurred when I was only nine years old.

I plotted and planned all day how I could sneak a bottle of wine from the liquor cabinet in my house. I remember that first sip of Boones Farm apple wine like it happened yesterday. Oh, that first sip of sweet nectar, that overwhelming sensation that coursed through my veins and tingled through my limbs. I had no idea that I was about to unleash hell's fury onto my life. That point of no return. Twenty minutes into my third drink my stomach began to turn, my skin discolored, and I would have it all back up - my first drunk puke! It was then that I realized I hadn't just opened a bottle of wine. I opened the never-ending predisposed condition of my disease. It didn't care that I was a child or that I would destroy the rest of my life chasing one bad decision after another. Although my first go at using was disastrous, I made a conscious decision to only remember the sensations and not the sickness.

I soon turned to more deviant behaviors such as stealing from mom's medicine cabinet. The crazy thing was I had no idea what those colored pills were. I never tried them - it was just the excitement I got from sneaking and stealing them. It was the overwhelming rush of mom's suspicion and my getting away with it that gave me pleasure. Soon it was more than just mom's pills. I grew into a kleptomaniac: my brother's cigarettes, my sister's jewelry, etc. I was hooked on the adrenaline rush. Soon I was scouring the neighborhood and stealing became a high in and of itself. My

neighbors' homes and garages satisfied my appetite. I remember my first real score. A case of Schlitz beer from my next-door neighbor's garage refrigerator.

I chased one destructive behavior after another. I was spiraling out of control and by the age of 16, I was using every day. The days of innocence were gone and little by little I became a recluse and partied alone, using way more often than my friends. The drugs became harder and more frequent, quickly moving from alcohol and pills to heroin and freebase cocaine. My love, passion, and addictions were now an everyday necessity. My disease of addiction was also changing my personality and soon I cared about nothing and nobody else but me. I completely abandoned my family and friends, and the young Bruce of yesterday was completely erased. I only made room in my life for more drugs; my deep pains of the past were comforted only by more painkillers. I suffered numerous near-death experiences due to overdoses and suicide attempts - all were just desperate attempts for temporary relief.

Altogether, I was in and out of treatment programs 36 times - one horrific moment after another. My insatiable need for ever-increasing highs resulted in a life of desperation and exhaustion. And it led to me becoming more heavily involved in organized criminal activities. I was an addict and a thief, and I was abusive to most of the women in my life, using prostitutes like punching bags and treating my wife the same. I thought I could change my life when I met her, but I was an animal, and anything or anyone that stood in the way of my using got steamrolled. Not even the precious gift of my daughter Kylee could stop my self-destruction and self-hatred from destroying everything.

I have now spent 70 percent of my life in mental and penal institutions, and it was in jail where I found God's saving grace. How could He accept, let alone love, such a misfit as me; evil at the core and toxic to everyone around me? When I surrendered my life to God in 2004, I was baptized in a 55-gallon drum of water by a fellow inmate/minister serving time with me. I remember that day well, although I didn't change much initially. I still used and went in and out of prison and treatment centers, but something did happen that

day - a seed was planted, and I started a long, exhausting journey searching for my recovery. Funny how God works. He didn't hate me when I let Him down like I used to hate Him. He forgave me and used every previous experience I ever had, and every relationship I had ever abused, to bring me to a place of forgiveness and love for others. It was in prison that I met Chaplain Potoka. I never saw what God was doing to bring me to this relationship with Chap. He would be the first real person I would care for as a man, so I would listen closely to every word when attending his classes, and even joined the prison church as an usher. I found I couldn't get enough of the good and practical wisdom I was getting in all the classes and programs that I attended. It was like drinking from a fire hose. I soon started replicating this teaching as I began to teach and counsel other inmates with histories of addiction. In this community of believers, I met my family of fellow misfits who, like me, had been rescued by Jesus. Boss-man, JJ, JD, Rusty, Shey, Ms. Cook, and many others would help me to put my ideas into practical usefulness for groups I was beginning to teach about recovery. My relationship with Jesus was measured in proportion to my relationships with these people and how they freely loved me and encouraged me.

I cannot tell you how hard it was to be abandoned by my own family. No one wanted me in their lives because I was using and destroying everything that ever mattered to them. It was here, in a South Carolina prison where God decided to mold me into the man I am today. I strive to teach men that all things are possible; God will make a way out of addictions for whoever will do the hard work of recovery. God wants recovery for them, and the relationship they have with themselves will determine how they look at others. Freedom from using is the sweet nectar of a transformed life. I desire to express the love of Jesus to the community I serve. This is my purpose and I long to be available to Him and others, continuing to live out my love for Jesus with men who were in broken lifestyles and relationships like me. I often use the tools of recovery to build a platform with others so I can create a meaningful dialogue that will bring them to the freedom and wholeness God created them to have, all because of one misfit like me coming to a right relationship with our Lord and Savior.

Thank you, mom, for always seeing me as a son when everyone else only saw an addict. Jim, you are much more than a stepdad - you are the greatest gift to me. I'm sorry for how our love started; I promise to care for you along the way. And Ms. Yates, for all your help and how you taught me to care and help those in need whether they deserved it or not – it was not for me to decide. You taught me how to be a peer-support specialist at its best. And Niki, for going the extra mile, as well as all the fellow peer-supports in SCDC – Mike, Regina, Sarah, and Sank – I am so proud to serve incarcerated men and women with you and help them to sobriety.

The call of God is often a pattern of coincidences in our lives that speak to our hearts with the realization that we are being pursued by God. God doesn't call us with words, but with evidence and a message encoded in the events of our lives. Sometimes this message does not make sense at first, and often it takes years before we can decipher its meaning - or even recognize that there is a message at all. When we become convinced that heaven has been in contact with our lives and we have been pursued and called by God with mercy and grace, then we must answer the call. But how do we answer? Simply put, we answer with the determination to change so that our life reflects the will of the One who has called us.

For me, however, this was not an easy process. Many obstacles in my life distracted me from discerning God's call. I was often trapped between false doctrine, social dysfunction, and the misdirection of popular culture. Instead of growing up in a nurturing and loving home that encouraged noble spiritual contemplations, I was born into an abusive family that challenged the notion of a loving God. My mother, who was a self-proclaimed "devout" Jehovah's Witness, was also a devout drug user and prostitute. Her life example did little to inspire in me a respect for God, His word, or the sacredness of life. Her influence instead left me confused about life's purpose and doubtful even about my self-image as a human being.

Contending with her moral poverty, however, paled in comparison to the struggles with financial poverty that ruled every sphere of my existence day in and day out. Poverty breeds desperation and desperation breeds crime. In time, I would attempt to lessen the pain and suffering of financial deprivation with criminal activity. Brainwashed by a culture of discontent that rules America's ghettos like a deranged tyrant, I was deceived into believing that my suffering could only be appeased by inflicting suffering on others. In other words, I could only stop being the victim when I took the initiative, went on the offensive, and victimized other people.

That decision lead me into an early life of crime. While other kids my age were playing the childhood game of cops and robbers, I became a real-life armed robber and a grand auto thief. My career as a car thief, however, was brought to an abrupt end at 14 years old when I wrecked a stolen vehicle, and my best friend who had come along for the ride died. Overnight I went from being an incorrigible youth to being declared a juvenile delinquent who was a menace to society. That point in my life set me on an irreversible path to prison.

Two years after that fatal car accident that took the life of my friend, I found myself sitting in an adult prison facility,16 years of age, with a 50-year grown man sentence. My failure to adjust to the juvenile justice system had simply placed me on a continued path of crime that became more severe with time. Something inside me was deeply disturbed and broken and I didn't know what it was. When I finally entered the adult prison system, I began to question God in a way that I had never done before. I asked, why was my life so filled with suffering and pain? Why had I been born to such an abusive and unloving mother? Why did my father abandon my mother and me as a child? Why did bad things always happen to me? And I was angry – with God, with the prison system, with myself.

 The common denominator to all my questions was human helplessness and desperation. The pain in my life revealed the fact that I was weak, helpless, and in need of God. Popular culture often promoted the notion of human independence and the idea that man was self-sufficient enough in his material knowledge to not need anyone - even God. My life was living proof that such a teaching was a false doctrine because as human beings we are supremely fragile creatures despite our advances in science, mathematics, medicine, and physics. My failures at being invincible to pain later proved irrefutable evidence that this man was inherently flawed and in dire need of God and a redeeming savior. However, it took some

time to decipher this message that God had encoded in the tapestry of my life.

The last thing I believed my painful life experiences to be was a communicated message from God. A message that was meant to enshrine the notion of human weakness and helplessness in my heart in preparation for my later acceptance of Him. Something was stirring in my mind though, there was something spiritual that was leading to a new awakening within me. Yet it would take another episode, another stint with false doctrine and failed theology before the light would finally shine into the midst of my spiritual darkness. When that moment arrived it would change everything, but it didn't arrive overnight. It would take more than two decades before many of my spiritual questions were to finally be answered and the writing on the wall of my spiritual timeline made clear so that God's presence in my life could be affirmed.

This was what I called my "wilderness moment," the time when I became diverted from God's purpose for my life by instructions from a false call. Before finding God's truth for my life in Christ, I wandered in the desert of Islamic theology for 28 years as a practicing Muslim. God, however, faithful in His pursuit of me, interrupted my delusions through a dream in which the resurrected Christ appeared to me. So completely revolutionary was the impact of this experience, that it not only compelled me to rethink my theology but to eventually leave Islam. It was during this phase of my life that the events began to form some coherent pattern that spelled out a divine message. A message that spoke of divine pursuit, eternal love, and human need.

The suffering, the abuse, and the pain all now made sense. I was now clearly able to see a spiritual framework where adversity had been used by God to induce disenchantment with the world and the doctrines of men. This prepared me to acknowledge my need for a loving God and Savior. God had used my painful life experiences to empty me of vanity and self-reliance so that He could fill me with the wisdom of an eternal perspective rooted in faith-centered gratitude.

 What began as a life in bondage to sin, anger, and depression; the lust of the eyes, lust of the flesh, and the sinful pride of life in this world, ended in spiritual freedom that was as boundless as eternity itself.

Having then made my commitment to follow Jesus Christ, I have now committed myself to convey the message of salvation to the world, especially focused on those who struggle emotionally where I once toiled. After more than 30 years of consecutive incarceration, with 8 years of that in solitary confinement for refusing to conform to prison rules, God has rescued me, redeemed me, and restored me to usefulness in His kingdom. God has given me a heart for those who suffer in ignorance and who are misinformed by false doctrine and have given up hope – I am a misfit, but I am also a miracle. To God be the glory!

HANNE GALLATIN

"When you were little, I did to you what Hannah did to Samuel. I dedicated you to the Lord's service." These were my dad's paraphrased words to me last Christmas as I was visiting my parents in my childhood home in Norway. "That is why you feel the way you do," he said, referring to my burden to do mission work. That beautiful statement from my father clarified a lot for me because as much as I wanted a traditional life with a family of my own and a nice home in the empty lot next to my parents, my greatest desire was and is to serve God. Even when I was young, I asked God if He would let me do something great for Him.

My childhood was quite unique in the best sense of the word because I had the absolute greatest opportunities to learn about God. The town I grew up in was very small with a large percentage of Christians. In fact, the town was so small that my class of 12 students was the largest in our school. Most of my friends were believers and are still today some of my closest brothers and sisters in Christ. My immediate family members were all dedicated followers of Jesus, and we learned the Word of God from both mom and dad as well as our grandparents. My grandfather was a traveling evangelist, and both my parents were Sunday school teachers. Our church was solid and Bible-believing. My friends' parents would talk about God and host Bible studies in their homes. School teachers would passionately share Bible stories in class, teach us hymns, and skip the chapters about evolution in science class. I loved God from a very young age, and as early as I understood more of what it meant to follow Him, I was all in with no hesitation.

Although I still had a hot temper and a flesh to deal with like the rest of us, I was one of those children who believed what the Bible said and lived according to it the best way I could. I felt strongly convicted whenever the other kids wanted to do something that was questionable, such as hide from the teacher if he briefly stepped out of the classroom, cheat on tests, or for some reason throw fruit on passing cars. And whenever we were walking outside in the dark, which happens often during the winter in Norway, I felt safe because I remembered the children's songs that said that Jesus was right there with me. I simply believed it.

If I were to place my younger self into a Biblical setting, it would have to be in the promised land. Not during Joshua's warfare, but during the time of the next generation who experienced peace in the land. I was safe. I was trusting. I knew nothing at all about war. As someone with a future in mission work, I was completely unaware that being on God's mission essentially meant going to war. When we continue the work of Jesus Christ, in sharing His good news that will set people free from Satan's power and reconcile them to God, we are actively waging war against the enemy: *"The reason the Son of God appeared was to destroy the works of the devil"* (1John 3:8). God in His wisdom knew that I needed to learn warfare in order to be a good and effective soldier in His army. This tender, trusting, and protected young girl was about to enter God's military academy.

My time in full-time ministry started in 2003 as I worked with a children's ministry for a mission organization in Norway. In 2008, I would take the leap of faith and travel to the USA to start an international music mission organization, *Gospel Through Music,* that would mobilize Christian musicians for short-term mission outreach. This spiritual military training started on a grand scale on my very first day of ministry work in 2003, and I think I'm partly still in this training program. In fact, I am not sure if the words military training covers the extent of it. It was a mixture of battles and deprivation. It has felt like boot camp and war all at once, and on location in the wilderness. This contrast to my upbringing was drastic. It was during this season of my life that everything was put to the test. This was when I fell the hardest, but also when the redemption was the sweetest.

God allowed many battles to come my way, and I often felt at a disadvantage because I had been stripped of what I personally and initially believed to be the great strengths for mission work, such as health, money, and a great network. My health was valuable to me because I thought I could be extra efficient and accomplish a lot of great things for God if I was healthy. Monetary resources were important to empower the missions' projects, and a large network was crucial to help make big things happen; a husband would be great for personal support and provision too. Instead, I found myself with a chronic illness in my body, I had no finances to rely on whatsoever, and because I had left Norway, I was isolated from my support network and there was no husband in sight. I felt like God withheld all of that from me.

In reality, God was teaching me the actual weapons of warfare found in His Word. He was teaching me to trust in Him alone, the Almighty General of the Hosts of Heaven. Simultaneously I needed to understand that I was unable to do effective ministry in my own strength. God was showing me that even if I was isolated from people, He was always near, and He demonstrated that He was a loving Father who would provide even when I couldn't. Let me share a few examples.

Throughout my health struggles, which have included severe fatigue for most of this time, it is nothing but a miracle to look back at how the music mission organization I began has shared the Gospel in  about 25 countries around the world - even in places where the gospel traditionally isn't welcomed. God has always provided financially for these projects, and for me personally as well when most of the time I had no knowledge of where money was going to come from. I remember one year an accountant did my taxes, and I had only made $10,000 that year. He asked me how I survived - truthfully, there were no explanations in the natural, but if God can multiply two fish and five loaves of bread to feed the five thousand, this is nothing to Him. I survived without any problem, and I never missed a meal or couldn't pay a bill, and God continues to be faithful in His provision to me today.

I want to share a rather personal story about how God has been so loving and caring, even in the small things in my life. I was getting ready to go to Norway for Christmas one year and was at a mall planning on getting ten one-dollar bottles of body lotions from Bath & Body Works to put in some gift bags for my friends. I didn't have ten dollars, but somehow, I knew that it was going to work out. As soon as I walk into the store, a lady who worked there greeted me and asked me if I would like to partake in a survey where they were testing some new scents. If I did, they would give me a ten-dollar gift card for the store. I, of course, said yes to that - excited about God's provision. When I finished the survey, they gave me the gift card for ten dollars, and they also added another coupon that would allow me to get a free body cream if I spent ten dollars in their store. I got the ten bottles I came there to get, and then I excitedly picked out a body cream that I liked the smell of. They rang me up and I walked out of the store. As Christmas was coming up, and I was low on cash, I started thinking about who I can give the body cream to. Suddenly I am startled by an internal voice that said, "No baby, that one is for you." It wasn't just the voice that startled me, but the fact that I was being called "baby." This single woman who was currently so lonely was just being called, "baby." I look into the bag to pull out the body cream I had chosen, and I noticed that it had the following words written on it in large letters: "PS, I love you!"

 Another time the Lord showed me how He is so present and caring in the middle of turmoil. I was lying in bed one evening, sick and completely overwhelmed. I needed confirmation that He was in control and that He was near. I called out to God, simply asking Him to show me that I was in His hands. Immediately the bed shook. Not just a little, but

much like an airplane experiencing turbulence. For me to get a physical example of Him holding me in His hands at that moment, was so uplifting that I instantly felt peace, and was able to fall asleep.

As much as God showed me how I could rely on Him in any situation, instead of on my own strengths and abilities, I still failed repeatedly. The situation was unfamiliar and disadvantageous. For a long time, I tried to fix my situation on my own. I would seek God, but if He didn't answer immediately or give me the answer I looked for, I frantically and anxiously tried to handle things my way; I was stressing out half the time. I would cry and complain about not having money and be paralyzed with fear when a deadline came up and I didn't know where the provision was going to come from. I would complain about not having a husband or good health and often doubting God's purpose and love for me. According to my reasoning, you see, having all of that would lead to me being more efficient in what He had called me to do.

The more I rebelled and chose my own way, the more I suffered the  consequences of that thinking. Through this all though, He gently, patiently, and sometimes firmly taught me His will and His way. He instructed me in obedience and repentance, and I got to experience His incredible and sweet mercy. And slowly, I was learning to do things His way and to rely on Him more and more.

Perhaps you were expecting another story of abandonment, addiction, delinquency, crime, or prison – my story is different, but much the same in the end. In ministry and on the mission field, I felt weak, made some bad choices, and struggled with whether I was still useful to God. Feeling weak, inadequate, and sometimes struggling emotionally and spiritually, I too had to learn to trust God with my present circumstances and future plans and wait for Him to be the provider for everything that I needed in life. There are no people who are doing effective ministry or serving on the mission field that are supermen or superwomen, strong in themselves, or even adequate without constant dependence on the Word of God and the presence of the Holy Spirit of God. God prepares us all by first breaking us and then remaking us, using all of our fears, scars, and difficult experiences to prepare us for what He has called us to do for His kingdom.

Today, I know that I could not have been effective on the mission field without this all-important season of growth in my life. The wilderness battles and subsequent victories adequately prepared me for doing His mission. This was crucial not just for me, but for the many souls that have been saved and seeds that have been planted through this ministry all around the world. If God didn't graciously mandate the military academy, I fear there would have been a far different outcome.

As unprepared as I was for the mission field 20 years ago, this extensive training has now given me a great passion to train and equip others for the mission field. Yes, God will probably have to take them to their own spiritual military academy, but I believe I can help better prepare young missionaries for what they can expect. My innocent faith as a young girl was put to the test in every way; and in the promises, the validity of His Word, and His character, God showed Himself strong in my life. Not only did my faith not crumble, but it was strengthened and deepened. I can tell you confidently: God is who He says He is. *"I had heard of you by the hearing of the ear, but now my eye sees you"* (Job 42:5).

JIMMY MCPHEE

I didn't grow up in a Christian home. Life was difficult. I remember

hearing angry voices and doors slamming in the night. People I thought I could trust came and went. The instability of my home and my feelings of insignificance gave rise to anger as I became a teenager. I experimented with drugs and broke the law. By the age of 19, I'd been arrested several times and served one year in prison for heroin possession. My time in jail didn't make me better - it made me bitter. Prison and prisoners are cruel, and I had to fight to survive. I witnessed wanton violence which hardened my view of the world. I came out angry and more broken than the youngster who had entered prison – and more dangerous. I was a time bomb disguised as a twenty-year-old kid!

Four months and seven days after leaving prison, the bomb exploded. I shot and killed a man and seriously injured another during an armed robbery. I was tried, convicted, and sentenced to die in the electric chair for my crimes. With my arms and legs shackled in heavy chains, I shuffled down the long row of cells called Death Row. Two stone-faced guards escorted me into a cell and slammed the door behind me. My stomach churned and my heart bled tears. Some day in the future there would be an execution, and I was the one condemned - I was 20 years old!

The last words of the judge rang in my ears, "May God have mercy upon your soul." I turned from the judge to my father who stood in the front row of the courtroom. I would carry the guilt and shame of that day for many years to come; it fueled my rage. As a youngster, I'd learned to channel my pain into anger. The rage I felt when my sentence was handed down drove me to declare war on a world that had rejected me.

The day after I was imprisoned, a little Japanese man arrived at my Death Row cell door. His duties as a librarian included delivering books to Death Row inmates, but he offered me something far more valuable than the stack of books in his hands. "My name is Frankie San," he said. "I love you, and Jesus loves you. He doesn't care what crimes you committed. He will forgive you if you let Him." I listened politely but cared nothing about my life, any other person's life, or a God I couldn't see. I was too blinded by hurt and rage. I now understand it was God's grace that after spending my 21st, 22nd, and 23rd birthdays on Death Row, the court re-sentenced me to life in prison with the possibility of parole. At the time, I wasn't all that grateful for the grace I'd been shown. I continued to be filled with rage, and I continued to reject God.

I adopted the prison culture of violence; I used drugs and alcohol to ease my pain. What I had abhorred as a first-time prisoner, I embraced as a lifer. I remained angry and assaultive, especially toward authority figures. At the age of 40, for my violent actions, I was locked away in solitary confinement for the duration of my sentence. Like that first day on Death Row, I again took inventory of my life. I'd spent 20 years in prison and had nothing to show for it but pain and devastation. Hopeless, I wrote to Frankie San, my old friend from Death Row, "I'm tired of my life. I desperately want something different, but I don't know what." He wrote back and shared the same words he had spoken in my cell 20 years before, "I love you, and Jesus Christ loves you. He doesn't care what crimes you committed. He will forgive you if you let Him. Give all your pain, anger, and brokenness to God, and He will heal you."

Trust was an issue, but I asked God to take what little life I hadn't destroyed and do with it what He would. I prayed, confessed my sins, and asked His forgiveness for all the pain I had caused. For the first time since I was a little boy, peace settled over my soul. I knew I'd never be alone again. I began to read the Bible. Over and over the words of truth spoke to me; the truth that changed my life is this:

> Jesus hung on the cross and rose on the third day so I and others like me could rise above our mistakes and live eternally free.
> I could entrust to Jesus the pain I'd caused my victims' families and the emotional hurt I'd imposed on my own family.
> Even though I lived in a solitary cell, I could walk away from the chains of anger, addiction, selfishness, and hate.

Little by little my thinking began to change. I read, wrote, and studied for hours each day. Life began to make sense as my heart and mind were transformed. Seven years later, after a total of 16 years in solitary confinement and 25 years in prison, God's mighty hand of grace again set me free; I was released to the prison general population. I continued to apply for release from prison, but most agreed I'd probably spend the rest of my life behind bars.

In the past 20 years, I've become a writer, speaker, teacher, and mentor to troubled younger prisoners and gang members. I've had the privilege of leading many men to the Lord as a servant leader in Kairos and JumpStart. In 2007, I was chosen as one of only 13 inmates to pursue a two-year Bible college education at Columbia International University: Kirkland Prison Initiative. Thanks to funding from private donors, I was trained to be a peacemaker and a missionary to the most dangerous prison yards in South Carolina. Imagine that – God transformed me, an angry violent murderer into a peacemaker! When God saved me, He gave me a purpose. With this purpose came the desire to bring honor and dignity to my life, my

victim's life, and my family, through my service to God.

The justice system said, "Execute him."

The prison system said, "Isolate him."

The parole system said, "Let him die in prison."

But once again God extended His mighty, loving hand. On March 18, 2020, after 45 years behind prison walls, He set this captive free. My parole had been granted! The JumpStart program where I once mentored young men on the inside would now be my residence on the outside, helping me successfully transition back into society. I formed a nonprofit ministry called *On THE ROCK Ministries* based out of Spartanburg, SC, where we have three ministry objectives: Share the hope of the Gospel through my testimony, bring light and hope to those I left behind that are still incarcerated, and reach at-risk youth to prevent their incarceration.

I grew up in Fairless Hills, PA, the youngest of five children. Two of my siblings were from my father's first marriage - one of them had Down Syndrome. My parents were both very loving; mom stayed home with the children and dad worked hard as a union electrician and was a good financial provider. Our family setting was a Christian home, going to church every Sunday morning and evening, Wednesday night, and whenever there was a special event – essentially, whenever the doors were open. I accepted Christ as a child but wandered away during my teen years. Sadly, two of my sisters suffered sexual abuse from my father; this created a lot of tension and sadness in our home. He always regretted what he did, would ask forgiveness and seek help but was never able to free himself from this bondage of sin.

My brother's friend introduced me to his friend Gerry when I was 15. We got married when I was 18 and he was 21. Gerry was employed at a Pennsylvania steel mill, and I worked as a medical assistant. We never attended church unless it included a nice roast beef lunch back at my mom's house. One day my sister Joy came over and talked to me about recommitting my life to Christ. I realized it was what I needed and so I prayed and asked God to forgive me for my sins. I started back attending a church in Trenton with a young pastor and wife from Kansas that I really liked. Gerry didn't attend.

One evening the pastor's wife called looking for me, but when Gerry answered the phone, Carol invited us to their home Bible study. He said no! But then he reluctantly started attending with me. I secretly started praying for Gerry, hiding my prayers in code in my journal so he wouldn't know what I was praying for. One Sunday night Gerry was going to play poker with some men from work, but the game was canceled so he went to church with me. The movie, *Thief in the Night* was shown, about Jesus coming back and taking Christians to heaven, and it spoke to Gerry; he realized he wasn't saved and that he would be left behind. He prayed and asked Jesus to forgive his sins and come into his heart and life. I was thrilled. Our pastor discipled us and Gerry started listening to sermons, reading Christian books, and studying the Bible.

One Sunday an invitation was given at the end of the service for anyone who felt God was calling them into ministry to come forward, and Gerry and I went up to the altar. We were willing to go wherever God would lead us in ministry. Gerry started to explore where he could go to study the Bible and prepare for full-time ministry. We had two sons and then through foster care, God brought a sweet little girl into our home, and we were able to adopt her. We had bought our first home in PA and then moved to a bigger house in Trenton, NJ; little did we know how God would use that house to finance our journey into ministry.

In 1987 we sold that house in New Jersey for a large profit, and Gerry, our three children, and I moved to Columbia, SC, so Gerry could attend Columbia Bible College. There were times when this

 was very scary, and we wondered if we did the right thing. But God always provided for our needs, sometimes at the very last minute. Gerry attended Bible college, worked part-time, and I worked full-time at the University of South Carolina. The children were active in swim teams, football, cub scouts, and other activities – our lives were hectic for the next three years.

After Gerry graduated from Bible college, he worked in the print shop at the school and delivered pizza while we looked for a ministry in which to serve. We interviewed at several churches, but nothing was working out. We started to feel discouraged because we had spent all the money we had made from selling our house, and we wondered when God would open a door for ministry. We were willing to go anywhere and do anything, but God wasn't providing a ministry position anywhere. Then out of the blue, we got a phone call from Charlesboro Baptist Church, in Kershaw, South Carolina.

One of the deacons had called the Bible college for names of graduates that would be interested in pastoring a church. At first, as Jim later told us, he crossed our name off their list because we had a "Yankee" sounding name, but when none of the other candidates were available, he unscratched our name and number, and called us. Gerry went there to preach, and they asked him to come back again to preach a trial sermon two weeks later. The second time I went with him. We drove through the small town of Kershaw, and I thought surely, we are almost there, but we just kept driving further out into the country and finally arrived. We aren't country people, and we wondered where the people lived who attended this tiny church.

When the church voted Gerry in as their new pastor, they asked when we could move into the parsonage and start as pastor – he asked, "is this Thursday OK?" We wanted to move into the area before school began the following week. From that first phone call, we were moving into the church parsonage within six weeks – God is an on-time God! Since it was a very small church and they could only pay $200 per week for our family of five, Gerry kept working at the Bible college and God provided a job for me in Lancaster in the insurance business. A few years into our stay in Charlesboro, we got a phone call from Pennsylvania asking if we were interested in coming back home to work in the financial planning business – pay started at $50,000 per year. It is tempting when you go into ministry and have no financial safety net under you, but we decided to trust

 God and continue in ministry. We stayed at that church for nine years. The people were very kind and good to us, and it was a good first experience for us in ministry. During our time in Charlesboro, the South Carolina Department of Corrections built Kershaw Correctional Institution right down the road from our community. Gerry started volunteering at the prison, not realizing that God was preparing him to one day be a chaplain there.

When our youngest son graduated high school, we decided it was time to move, so we moved to Charlotte, NC. Gerry was then working

as a clinical coordinator for Mentor, a therapeutic foster care agency that works with children with emotional dysfunction, and I started continued working in medical insurance claims. Once again, God provided for our needs. After visiting some larger churches, we started attending a small Baptist church in the Ballantyne area of Charlotte. About six months later when the pastor died of cancer the church asked Gerry if he would consider pastoring and he took the position. While in Charlotte we became volunteers with El Roi Ministry, a residential home for women who had suffered childhood sexual abuse. When that ministry was in danger of shutting down because the director got cancer, we volunteered to move the ministry into our home. I was the full-time director, and we had a curriculum that helped the women work through the damage of their developmental trauma of sexual abuse, introduced them to a personal relationship with God, and help them work toward successful independent living.

 Six years later we felt the need to leave the church in Charlotte and wondered where God was directing us next; it was once again a very stressful time for us. As usual, God provided a ministry for us at Lois' Lodge, a faith-based maternity home. I was the main residential director, working and living at the home with the girls through the week and going home on weekends. I really enjoyed working with these young women. We were so glad they chose life for their babies. I accompanied many of them to the hospital as they delivered their babies and began their lives as new parents. What a wonderful experience it was for the next year and a half. After our time at the maternity home, I began working at a Christian recovery home for women seeking a godly solution to their alcohol or drug addiction. I provided a daily structured living program, had regular Bible studies with them, and mentored them in life skills. It was so encouraging to work with these women in crisis as they recovered and went back home clean and sober and able to lead productive lives. Our next adventure was to assist with the Zacchaeus House, a transitional house for men leaving prison and wanting a successful transition back to society. Next, we moved to Rock Hill, SC, and helped begin The Life House, a

new maternity home for women in difficult or crisis pregnancies. I then volunteered at Palmetto Women's Center, a pro-life ministry that encourages pregnant women to choose life for their babies and choose a godly life for themselves.

I now work in home health care, ministering to elderly people who are sick and trying to recover physically so they can stay living in their own homes. It is a Christian organization, so I am able to pray and read God's Word with them. I also volunteer at the Goshen House, a transitional home for women who are going through a crisis time in their lives and are working toward healing and transitioning back to independence. I am so thankful that God has provided all of these opportunities to serve women, loving on them and helping them through difficult times, showing them that God can change their hearts and lives.

My advice to my sisters in Christ is even when it is scary, you may feel like you're not equipped to help people in need. If you know God is leading you, go for it. You won't regret it. God doesn't call the qualified, He qualifies the called. And He will give you wisdom and strength to complete the task and you will be blessed – and so will they!

EDWARD MCKNIGHT

I grew up in a normal middle-class family with a focus on education. My mother is a retired principal, and my father was a retired chef/supervisor. My parents had built a strict family structure and I was taught the importance of going to church; church attendance was not an option. I attended Catholic School for eight years where I developed a love for reading and writing. I was raised much like a single child, having two siblings that are much older than me: a brother nine years older and a sister 20 years my senior. With no other siblings in the home to interact with, I was essentially a loner.

 Born in South Carolina and raised in Georgia, my life outside of the home was active with sports at the YMCA, Jr-high school sports, and a few high school activities.

Throughout my later childhood and into my youth, I was constantly involved in inappropriate activities, and I was sexually promiscuous. I also was experimenting with drugs and alcohol at an early age – smoking weed as early as eighth grade with a friend, thinking that it was cool. As I look back on my life, that started opening the door for other drugs. Alcohol was an early addiction for me after I started drinking when I was about ten years old. We didn't have alcohol in my home, but a girlfriend's parents had plenty of alcohol at their house, so it was easy to find something to drink. My parents noticed one day that I was acting strangely and decided to take me to the doctor. The doctor asked me to count backward from 100. I got down to 90 and went blank - I just could not remember the rest.

These behaviors didn't happen in a vacuum; there were a lot of dynamics that drove my dysfunction. I was molested several times as a young boy, the first time when I was about eight years old. The offender was a local youth that was 16 years old. I remember him taking off my clothes and molesting me, and then putting baby powder on my genitals and rectum, as though that made everything ok. Thinking about it now, I want to throw up. I have forgiven him, but it will always be a scar that marked my adolescence. Recently, I spoke to my brother about what happened to me, and he said that the same youth did the same thing to him, but without the baby powder.

At the age of ten, I was molested again at the Boy's Club. Several of us boys were playing in a room, and an older boy came in the room, grabbed me, and began to molest me. The other boy took off running, but not to get help for me. I remember being in that room all alone with that boy for what seemed like an eternity. He was at least six years older than me, and I was helpless against his assault. When I got home, I told my mother what had happened, and she reported it to the director of the Boy's Club. My mother also found out where the older boy lived and went to their home to confront him. She spoke with the young man in the presence of his mother, and the young man denied everything, which was not surprising. I'm not sure why she didn't call the police, but back then everybody wanted to keep things hidden. Here, I am 59 years old, and I remember every bit of that story as if it was yesterday. I am a Misfit.

I believe that seeds were planted in my life on those two occasions that caused me to struggle with homosexual desires and feeling for many years to come. In my case, it was a learned behavior. I was naïve and innocent as a child. I began to have strong feelings by the age of 13. I remember inviting a friend over to the house, and while we sat at the breakfast table, I began to have feelings toward him. He looked at me and asked, "Why are you looking at me like that?" I did not know how to answer him. Because of shame and not wanting anyone to know my struggles, I never shared my struggles and my feelings with anyone. I pretended to be straight and hid my true feelings by playing sports, having a girlfriend, and pursuing my education goals. I was wearing masks to cover on the outside who I was becoming on the inside. Honestly, I did not know how to deal with my feelings or how to receive the grace of God to be delivered and free from confusing and conflicting thoughts and desires. I had accepted Christ into my life, but I still struggled and did not know how to receive God's love and grace to change. I continued to consume alcohol and smoke weed regularly and when I turned 18, my life changed drastically.

I came home from school one afternoon and there was a Church of Christ Minister in my home. Getting right to the point, the Minister asked me, "If you were to die right now, where would you go?" I told the Minister that I would go to Hell. When he asked me if I would be interested in going to Heaven, I said, "Yes Sir!" He then led me through the *Romans Road to Salvation*, a technique using only the Bible's book of Romans to explain how to come to salvation. We went immediately to the Church of Christ where I was baptized. The Church of Christ taught me the importance of reading and studying my Bible. One of the key scriptures I had to memorize was (II Timothy 2:15 KJV). "Study to show thyself approved unto God, a workman that needeth not to be ashamed, rightly dividing the word of truth." I did not agree with some of the doctrines and practices of the Church of Christ, but I believe God used that Minister and that denomination to introduce me to Christ and teach me to walk in His ways. I was raised in the church, but I was not introduced to Christ until that afternoon.

There are a lot of churches that are not teaching Christ or giving a salvation message. How tragic to be in church and never have the opportunity to hear the gospel message of rescue and redemption. I later would attend *Overcoming By Faith*, a Four-Square Church in Savannah Georgia. There I received a true change and conversion, and I received the Baptism of the Holy Spirit and a true revelation of Christ. I still had my struggles, but I was beginning to understand God's grace. Although I received Christ and received the Baptism of the Holy Spirit, I was still conflicted with feelings of same-sex attraction. To cover my feelings and attractions, I once again engrossed myself in deflecting activities. I graduated from college, went through R.O.T.C., was commissioned as a 2nd Lieutenant in the active military, and graduated from seminary with two master's degrees before the age of 30. Yet I still struggled with my sexual identity and understanding of who I was in Christ.

I thought maybe marriage would solve this problem and I could then live for Christ in a healthy marital relationship. Before I married my first wife, she knew that I had struggled with same-sex attractions

and behaviors. She said it did not matter to her as long as I was now a new creation in Christ. The past was the past. Our marriage lasted for only three years. One blessed result of that marriage was the birth of our beautiful baby daughter. I was deceived into believing that it was Ok to continue living a homosexual lifestyle. I thought that it was my battle and mine alone. I decided I was going to live life my way and not God's way. I wanted to live a lifestyle pleasing to my flesh. My ex-wife told me she believed I would eventually change, but I wanted to move on, and I wanted a divorce. The divorce was granted and for the next eight years, I lived a promiscuous lifestyle. I was operating as a hypocrite - I was pastoring a church, and counseling other people, yet doing drugs and living a life of sin. God has a way of allowing us to hit rock bottom. But this wasn't rock bottom yet!

Sin will take you places you never thought you would go, and I never thought that I would be introduced to crack cocaine. I was living in Asbury Park, New Jersey in a house being rented by a gay couple. God tried to stop me - I had a dream warning me not to move into this house. In the dream, there were snakes all over the house and in the apartment that I was going to move into, but I did not take heed. It was only a few months after moving in that I was introduced to crack cocaine by my gay partner. "Preacher man, meet crack!" Crack quickly became my drug of choice. When I ran out of money buying the drug, I would sell things that I owned to get more crack. I even started to rent out my car for more crack, and eventually lost it – to crack. I lost everything! My dad had to come and get me from Asbury Park and take me back to South Carolina. I was ashamed. As I was riding back home with my dad, I finally began to think about how I was losing control of my life. How did I end up in this predicament? How did end up a homeless crack addict? Maybe this was rock bottom? Not yet!

For the next year, my parents assisted me in receiving drug counseling and life assistance. I eventually found a job and completed one year of CPE (Clinical Pastoral Education). This was just a cover-up. I was still living a promiscuous sexual lifestyle and continuing to live as a functional crackhead. I graduated from CPE and was offered a job with the South Carolina Department of Corrections at Lieber Correctional Institution as a chaplain. This job only lasted one year because of state budget cuts. I believe God allowed me to work only a year because I was living an ungodly lifestyle and God wanted men of godly character. After the job as chaplain ended at Lieber, I was offered a pastorate for the United Methodist Church. I was still promiscuous and refused to live a life of godly character. The harder my head and heart became, the harder the fall would be.

As I was pastoring, I again began lending my car out to drug dealers and received crack cocaine in return. My downfall began when I rented my car out to a drug dealer, who then told me he was going to kill me because I reported him to the police after he did not return my car to me. The dealer came to my church parsonage where I lived and left a note stating that I was a dead man. I panicked! I had to call my church District Superintendent and tell him that my life was being threatened, and he told me to take a few clothes and leave town immediately. I resigned from my church and decided to move to Atlanta, Georgia. My parents gave me $250 and put me on a bus to Atlanta. My first year in Atlanta consisted of living in shelters and eating what was given to me which was mostly soup at homeless ministries. I never imagined that I would have to sleep on floors and smell the feet of men. What a humbling experience. I thank God that he allowed me to experience this. Finally, rock bottom? No, not yet!

There was still one more step down, one more experience that I would have to go through before I would surrender to a life of holiness and godly character. There was a guy I met my first year who showed me another lifestyle of getting crack and living to get high. We would steal and do drugs and live in flea-bag motels. I finally got tired of living in filth and living a life of sin. I told him that we needed to go our separate ways before we ended up in jail. He did, but God was beginning to get my attention. Sometimes you just have to get sick and tired of being sick and tired. Finally, real rock bottom!

I began to seriously pray and ask God to lead me and guide me. Truth be told, He was trying to lead me, but I wasn't willing to follow. God would soon lead me to a ministry called, *Clarity*. *Clarity* was a men's ministry where we worked and received classes to grow spiritually. *Clarity* was the beginning of my finding God's purpose for me. The founder of *Clarity* had a spiritual mentor, Pastor Seven, who would become my spiritual mentor as well for the next eight years. I lived at *Clarity* for one year, and then I was invited to start working with Pastor Seven in a ministry called, *7 Bridges to Recovery*, and I said yes. This was the ministry that brought true change to me, and I wanted to in turn learn to be a disciple of Christ and to make disciples of other men. God had rescued me, and I wanted to be someone who helped rescue other men just like me.

 This ministry is designed for the misfits of society. When I first went to *7 Bridges to Recovery*, it was only serving about five men at a time. We would feed the homeless every day throughout the week, and on Saturdays, we would have our biggest outreach where we would go to the part of town called the Bluff. This is where the worst of the worst, the neediest of the needy, and the most lost of the lost lived. The Bluff was known as a haven for drugs, crime, hopelessness, and despair. We would pass out lunches and minister the salvation message, and as able, we would train willing men and women to work with us in ministries of hope and deliverance. We were misfits making disciples of other misfits to the glory of God.

7 Bridges began to grow over the years, and I became Pastor Seven's, right-hand man. We grew from one residential home to three homes, sponsored a church that housed 100 women and children, and developed a cutting-edge ministry feeding thousands throughout the week all the while making disciples for Christ. I was a part of *7 Bridges* for eight wonderful years of my life. Out of the blue, I received a call from my mother asking if I would consider coming back to South Carolina. I prayed about it, and I had peace about coming back to South Carolina and pursuing pastoring – this time as a true man of God. I received the blessing of Pastor Seven to leave Atlanta, and I began filling out the paperwork to be reinstated in the

United Methodist Conference. It was September of 2016 when I traveled back to South Carolina for the next chapter of my life. God began to open doors for me that I never thought possible.

Not only was I reinstated as a pastor, but God opened the door for me to once again be a chaplain for SCDC. I am at this time the Senior Chaplain at Lee Correctional Institution, which is considered by many to be one of the worst prisons in South Carolina. Not only did I become a pastor and a chaplain, but God also gave me a beautiful wife and stepchildren. My wife knows my past but loves me unconditionally - much like my Lord and Savior does. We were married in August of 2017, and I now have a godly partner in life and ministry. God has also restored to me my daughter, who is now married to an awesome young man, and we now have a beautiful relationship that only God could have designed. I never thought that God would grace me like this. He gave me back everything the enemy had stolen from me and more. God has restored His character in me. I am reminded of a saying: The anointing will get you there, but the character will keep you there. God loves Misfits like me!

RICARDO & IVY SHERARD

Ricardo - I was born in 1971, addicted to heroin. My mother loved

ADDICTED BABIES

me, but she had many problems in her life – heroin being one of them. I didn't really know my father, so, my grandparents ended up raising me. My grandfather was a hard worker who loved to smoke weed. My grandmother was a devoted Christian who made my grandfather and I go to church every Sunday. My grandfather would make me sit by him, pull his knife out and tell me that I better not move.

By 1982, I was heavy into rapping and break dancing in my Adidas suit and a pair of tennis shoes that my grandparents bought me, but I wanted to wear a different color every day, so I started stealing. By 1987, I had graduated from petty theft to become a full-time criminal. I would do anything to stack my pockets with money. I was part of a group that would steal cars in Columbia and sell them to a chop shop in Charlotte. One night when we needed gas money; I attempted to rob a young man walking on the street and I ended up killing him. Although my behavior made me feel all grown up, I was only 15 years old – and a murderer.

Ivy - I was born in Charlotte, NC, in 1970 to a Marine Corps Drill Sergeant father from Philadelphia and a mother who was a schoolteacher from Beaufort, SC. I had a happy childhood until my parents split up when I was around three or four years old. My mother and I moved in with my aunt, uncle, and cousin in Columbia, SC – I wasn't sure where my father was at the time. While living with

them, I met Ricardo. He was the little boy across the street who would just "appear" whenever I would come outside in the yard to play.

He would come over and mess up my mud pies and find a way to make me cry and run in the house. But, minutes later he would return to our yard and wait for me to come out and I would eventually play with him again despite the warnings from my aunt to leave "that boy" alone. One day, he even went inside our house and grabbed my cousin's BB gun and shot me point blank in the behind. Later he tried to explain that it was his expression of love. My mother and I eventually moved from the Greenview neighborhood across town and I attended a new school. My life was a little confusing to me at the time because I didn't know anyone there, I missed my dad, and my mom was working so much that I barely got to see her.

I was around eight years old when the relationship between my mom and me began to get strained. I would be in school during the day, home alone in the evenings because my mom worked the night shift, and I would spend the weekends with my aunt and uncle. I loved going to their house because I felt like their home was more of a family with my uncle being present in the house, and they loved me like their own. Meanwhile, I would always look for the boy across the street, Ricardo. My aunt was close friends with his family, especially his mom and aunt, so we would go back to the old neighborhood to visit. I grew fond of his mother and grandma, so whenever I would go over there, I would ask about Ricardo who was never home. "Oh, he's out in the street somewhere!" they would reply, so I would just say, "Ok, tell him I asked about him and hopefully see him next time."

This went on for several years, not seeing each other. When I was in the 8th grade, I began having sex with a football player from school who I considered my boyfriend. One night he decided to put me in a situation where he brought one of his football buddies into his bedroom for the three of us to have sex, and they forced me to do so. Afterward, my so-called boyfriend stopped talking to me for a few days and I didn't understand why. Then, one night while my mom was at work, I got a knock on my door. Thinking that it was my boyfriend, I opened it and four guys pushed their way in and gang raped me. The main guy was the one that my boyfriend had brought to the house before for me to have a threesome with.
I didn't call the police, and I didn't tell my mom or family members because I thought that they would blame me for it and say that I deserved it. At this time, Ricardo had a reputation for fighting and hurting people and I was seeking revenge. I would go to my aunt and

uncle's house and look for Ricardo but couldn't find him. I would even look for him at the skating rinks, game rooms, and local movie theater but to no avail. I began feeling depressed after that and I also had low self-esteem. I wasn't interested in school because I got picked on a lot because of my worn-out clothes and shoes - not to mention the rumors about me. I kept looking for Ricardo to come and make things better for me, but he was nowhere around. We reconnected and talked about life in general, not knowing that he would commit murder and be sentenced to life in prison soon after that.

Ricardo - I was arrested and placed in the county jail. Being that I was still a juvenile, I was housed in the women's wing of the jail. Every day women would come down to my cell for sex. I thought I was being a man knocking off women 25, 30, and 40 years old. The truth is, I never realized that I was actually being sexually molested by these women.

In 1988, while waiting to go to court for my murder charge, I met a student from Columbia Bible College who was doing jail and prison ministry. He visited me almost every Sunday morning, and we soon became friends. He shared his faith in Jesus with me, telling me how a right relationship with God through Jesus Christ would bring forgiveness for my sins, adoption by God into His family, and the desire and power to live a new life. Despite my past, I could have meaning and purpose in my life even while incarcerated. One day he asked me if I would consider giving my life to Christ. I asked him if it would get me out of this jail. He said Christ has the keys to heaven and hell, and he can open any door He chooses. So, I said yeah, I want Him in my life. He prayed the sinner's prayer with me, and I verbally accepted Christ as my Lord and Savior. But I was no more saved as a prostitute on Saturday night. When I went to court, I pled guilty to murder and the judge sentenced me to what I thought was eternal life in prison - plus 20 years. On the next visit with Gerry, he assured me the judge could not sentence anyone to eternity anywhere. But it was for the rest of my natural life, plus 20 years.

By 1992, at 21 years old, I had already served five years of my sentence. My reputation for violence had spread. I had to fight on the street, and I fought in prison. I would rob other prisoners as well as some officers. I was known for hurting people and causing a lot of blood. People started calling me "Damu" which means blood in Swahili. I really didn't care about anyone because I was sentenced to Life+20 years. I didn't feel like I would ever get out. So, I lived my life by my rules - make money and make people fear me. I didn't care anything about God or religion. In fact, I felt like religions only separated people. For example, if I was a Christian and the guy next to me was a Muslim, we could not accept what the other believed, because the most basic foundational principle in each religion is that You Shall Not Serve Other Gods. In my mind, this created division among the people. So, I started studying Egyptology, Black history, the culture and religion of Ethiopia, and socialism around the world.

In my 15th year of incarceration, I was in a cell on lockup when four officers had just finished roughing me up. I used to call it fighting but it wasn't a fight - they had on pads, helmets, and shields and all I had on was my underwear. After they left, I heard one of them say, "Damu", and when I turned around, he sprayed me in my face with some Mace, better known as Capshaw pepper spray. It was burning so bad that I could hardly take it. The water in my cell had been turned off and the only liquid I had was the water in the toilet – which was also full of urine and feces. After about 12 minutes my skin felt like it was pealing. So, I got on my knees and started putting that human waste on my face. All those years that my grandparents made me sit and listen to the word of God came back in an instant. While I was putting this excrement on my face to stop the burning, I was calling out to God and asking Him to get me out of this mess. I was telling Him that I don't want this life no more. Out of the blue, a lady whom I had never

seen before came to my cell and said, "Ricardo stop doing that!" I said I couldn't because I am burning. She said she was going to get the keys and take me to the shower to clean off. She took me to the shower and from that day I never committed any more crimes or violated any more institutional regulations. My life had been transformed.

Ivy - Things changed for me when my mother and I moved to Beaufort, SC, to be near my grandparents; except for the fact that my mom then had a boyfriend who I really didn't like. After a trying year there, things got so bad that I moved to Philadelphia to live with my father. Philadelphia was great to me! A new place where nobody knew my past, new friends, new school, and most of all, I'm with my daddy!! West Philly High School was a lot of fun. After completing the 10th grade, I went back to my aunt and uncle's house in SC for the summer, and I ran into Ricardo at a summer concert at the community park, then we lost contact again. I went back to Philly and graduated in '88 with high grades, was a popular cheerleader, softball player, and student government representative - all things that I couldn't dream of doing in South Carolina. Then my mother got sick in my senior year, and I returned to SC right after graduation to take care of her until she died in 1989. It was hard to deal with her death and other issues in my life at that time. In the meanwhile, I was working a lot and trying to block out my damaged emotions. I ended up moving back to Philly where I met a guy who eventually became the father of my son. Our relationship didn't work out, so I moved back to SC.

I moved into my aunt and uncle's house again, this time with my son. I would sometimes visit Ricardo's grandmother and mom, but I didn't have any contact with him. I would just ask about him and tell them to tell him that I asked about him. In 2004, I had a relationship that ended badly, and Ricardo's grandmother knew about it. So, one day when she went to visit him in the prison, she asked him if he remembered me, and he said that he did; she gave him my address and he wrote to me. We began writing at least three letters a day to each other, and I began visiting him at Kershaw. We fell in love and eventually began talking about marriage even though we weren't sure if he would ever be paroled and come home. It was our faith in God that we held on to. Months later, I caused us to break up because I was being unfaithful, and Ricardo decided to stop speaking and writing to me. I was ashamed and hurt because I had hurt him and lost his trust. Because of that mistake, he met someone else, got paroled, and married that woman. I was crushed but had to accept the fact that I made a mistake, and he had moved on with someone else.

That is when I decided to rededicate my life to Christ – I was smoking weed, drinking, and being promiscuous, and was overall unhappy with my life. Ricardo was unhappy in his life too. We began talking and seeing each other again. He later divorced and when it was finalized, we quickly got married in 2015. We've been happy ever since, and we rarely do anything apart from each other. We worked together, owned a business, and started doing ministry to others as a team. We have now been married for seven years - our proudest accomplishment is being Chaplains together with Christ Central Ministries and serving right in our community with the Word of God, prayer, housing, meals, clothing, food – and lots of love.

Ricardo - God had changed my life forever. All the things I had heard about Jesus came rushing back to my mind - I surrendered my life to Christ and started to live a transformed life. I was soon transferred to Kershaw Correctional Institution, and to my surprise, that bible college student from the county jail was their chaplain. I attended church and Bible study groups and went into training for ministry within the prison setting. I learned to study the Bible, practice it, then teach, and preach the Word and minister to hurting people -

instead of hurting people. I went before the parole board when I had served 20 years and received conditional parole. I had to be given a psychological exam to see how I would adjust to society, and they failed me and took away my parole. Two more years at Kershaw Bible College, then I went again before the parole board for the second time. I was immediately rejected for parole – then a miracle happened. One of the parole board members called Chaplain Potoka and said I needed to request a new hearing and told him to work with me to get me ready to go home. That was in November 2009, and a new hearing was scheduled for January 2010. I was again granted conditional parole upon passing the psychological exam – and was released from the South Carolina Department of Corrections in March 2010. To God be the glory!

I've been out of prison now for nearly 13 years. I thought in my simple mind that I would have a prison ministry, going back inside the prisons ministering the Word of God. But God showed me that there are people in society who are mentally/psychologically confined. God's call to ministry is a call to preparation, so my wife Ivy and I have been trained as Community Chaplains, working to help brothers and sisters break the chains of addiction, criminality, chronic homelessness, hunger, and low self-esteem. So now I am a misfit that God uses to help other misfits fit successfully back into society. My question to the reader, my fellow misfit - what are you going to do??? Chaplains Ricardo & Ivy Sherard reporting for duty!

"Let the redeemed of the Lord say so." (Psalm 107:2).

My story begins in Cincinnati as the oldest of five children in a middle-class suburban German family (Holocher). We were very involved in our church, with Dad on the church council and the evangelism team. Mom sang in the choir and helped with Vacation Bible School. Everyone received awards for attendance, but we did not read the Bible together or pray as a family. I was baptized as an infant and confirmed at age 12. I believed God was Father (creator) and that Jesus was His only begotten Son who died and rose again. The Holy Ghost was only known to me in the creeds. We had "religion" but not a relationship with God. I knew of God but had no personal dealings with Him.

I was a good student and a member of the Honor Society at school. Although I spent a lot of time enjoying the outdoors: camping, scouting, softball, and being with my friends, my favorite activity seemed to be doing whatever it took to get Dad's attention. The "whatever I had to do" led to a lot of time-outs in the corner. I was jealous of my sister, which was displayed clearly in my rebellious and argumentative nature. As Holochers we were prideful – one of the best families in the neighborhood, church, and school. Unfortunately, our "always-super" family imploded and exploded simultaneously in my senior year of high school.

"For who makes you different from anyone else? What do you have that you did not receive?" (1 Corinthians 4:7).

My parents divorced and we all "fell down." *"If you think you are standing firm, be careful that you don't fall."* (1 Corinthians 10:12). Since I already felt that I was different and difficult, my immature reasoning led me to seek male companions who wouldn't want marriage, therefore, no divorce. I was self-reliant rather than God-reliant. When I was in college I walked away from the church, and I alienated myself from God. I did manage to graduate with a BA in Elementary Education - and an advanced degree in destruction. I had way too many "not husband material" partners, a rape, and an abortion.

"So, whoever knows the right thing to do, and fails to do it, for him it is sin." (James 4:17)

I was deceived! I was defending my "alternate lifestyle" of destruction until age 29. Then I stopped running and dabbling in drugs, being warned by prophet Jeremiah, *"Can a man hide himself in secret places so that I cannot see him?"* (Jeremiah 23:24). The big 30 was staring me in the face. Wow, I had to regroup fast. I felt I needed to find a responsible partner or have a child with a sperm donor. Although my mother was remarried and living in Florida, she was able to persuade me to, *"Trust in the Lord with all your heart, and lean not unto your own understanding."* (Proverbs 3:5).

Using my college education, I was teaching in a Montessori school. Two things motivated me to want to teach in that model of  education. First, Montessori philosophy allows children considerable freedom of choice, as opposed to the strict upbringing I had received. And second, I could probably even breastfeed my child in the classroom - always preparing for the worst-case scenario. I had lots of low self-esteem! Fortunately, I married a great man, the father of two children, and by age 34 I went from having no children to being the mother of three! During these years, I was the director of a Christian tutoring/counseling center called, Growth Ways. It was a great experience for me, but we were only nominal attendees of a non-denominational church. Without the necessary focus and prayer, the marriage gradually dissolved. Another "I know what I'm doing decision" that seemed right. I moved my eight-year-old son Shawn with me to Charlotte, North Carolina, to live near my mother and youngest sister.

Once again, unmarried and living with a man (notice a pattern here!) my mom and sister assured me that they were going to pray for me every day for a year. I boldly responded, "Don't stop then! If God wants to get my attention, He will have to hit me over the head with a 2 by 4." And praise God – He did! I had a Damascus road-type experience. My youngest sister would kindly, but persistently, invite me to Bible studies, to which I'd reply, "If I want to go, you'll be the first to know." So, the day I heard these words come out of my mouth, "Yes, I'll go," I knew the Holy Spirit was answering, and so I agreed to go. This was definitely a move of God.

Sitting on a couch with the group of women taking notes from a video, Beth Moore led us through a study called, "*Breaking Free.*" I was hit over the head with that 2 by 4! I don't know how, but I ended up face-down on the carpet, sobbing uncontrollably! When I finally stood up, I asked, "What is this place?" They told me it used to be a faith-based home for women dealing with substance abuse issues but was 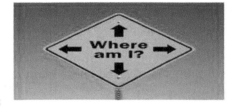 now closed because no one was available to work nights. Immediately I committed, "I'll stay." And stay I did until the ministry closed five years later. It was and is one of the most intense things that has happened to me!

Still teaching school, I initially stayed overnight only, but the desires of my heart changed. I resigned at the end of that school year and was able to stay and grow up spiritually, at RRR (Redeemers Recovery Ranch). God had me right where He wanted me - His plan, my purpose, my mess, His message. "*I have blotted out, as a thick cloud, thy transgressions and as a cloud, thy sins: return unto me; for I have redeemed thee.*" (Isaiah 44:22). "*For when we were yet without strength, in due time Christ died for us.*" (Romans 5:8). I rededicated my life to Christ, repented, and was baptized. "*Therefore, if anyone is in Christ, he is a new creature; the old things have passed away, new things have come.*" (2 Corinthians 5:17). And now the truly exciting part of my life began. I was spiritually hungry and thirsty.

One afternoon a friend came by asking where I had been. I told her I was having an affair. Unmarried, she looked at me very puzzled. I was having a love affair with Jesus; engrossed in His Word. I prayed earnestly for my son's recovery from heroin addiction. Praise God, he soon agreed to go to a Christian recovery center; was saved, baptized, and his new life began. Our God is a God of second chances! Another answered prayer came when I met Sandy through a mutual friend in ministry. On our second dinner date, I saw his lips moving, but couldn't hear his voice. But I heard God's voice! He spoke to me very clearly, "This is the man I have for you." You can believe - so I believed! We soon married, and another adventure began!

Sandy had studied under Chuck Colson in the Centurions program of Prison Fellowship. In response to an assignment, he wrote out his vision for a men's transitional house. He had been teaching classes in Kershaw Correctional Institution and overseeing some men who reentered society under the direction of El Roi Ministries. Unfortunately, my involvement in that ministry was put on hold due to a new diagnosis of breast cancer calling for surgery, chemo, and radiation, A woman I had not previously met approached me one Sunday after church and said she felt called to talk to me in, so in one of the classrooms I told her about my health issue. She laid hands on me and prayed. This was not common practice in the Well of Hope Lutheran Church, but soon here I was, *the woman at the well*" at the church called the Well, being made well. Isn't God good?

The next months it was as though I was pregnant. I knew I was going to be healed physically, but month by month, reading the Bible more each day, and praying fervently, I was birthing a new level of faith. Little did we know that El Roi Ministry was selling some of the properties they had been gifted during this time. They had a proposal for Sandy and me - would we be interested in living in a house where incarcerated men could live after release from prison while transitioning back into society? HELLO!! Thank You Jesus... and so the hunt began. We were both searching online for a suitable property for this ministry when Sandy found an ideal house. Disappointed, I had to point out the words "contract pending" for that house. But God! The sale contract fell through, and the ideal house became available again, and Sandy and Chaplain Potoka walked in and KNEW that was the place God was providing.

After some renovations, the Zacchaeus House soon opened. As directors of the home, we lived upstairs and over the next five years, more than 100 men entered that home directly from prison. They secured identification, found work, attended church, went to Celebrate Recovery, had weekly bible studies, met with volunteers for weekly fellowship dinners, and participated in community service projects. Secure in their identity in Christ, surrounded by a loving community of staff and volunteers, most transitioned into society successfully. These were undoubtedly some of the best years of my life!

Sandy retired from his lifelong career as an east coast and local truck driver. He was right where God wanted him and most certainly where he wanted to be. God had equipped me to be his wife and ministry partner. While Sandy was attending online seminary through Broad River Academy, we were blessed to attend an LCMC (Lutheran Churches in Mission Conference) in Dallas where one of my sisters and her daughter lived. Later we traveled to Alabama to bring an art display to their church, and I was able to visit my stepson and stepdaughter. We retreated to Oak Island several times courtesy of friends. My life had become one of abundant blessings!

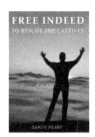

And Kershaw prison! Kershaw Bible College as we referred to it. Seeing the Spirit move as 50+ plus incarcerated men in a prison chapel sang *Way Maker* with such freedom and joy was an experience I will always remember. Five years passed – and then so did Sandy. (He was ready of course, but I wasn't). But I will always be grateful for the time God gave us together. A book of some of his many poems is soon to be published and available on Amazon, "*Free; Indeed, To Rescue the Captives.*" Now he is with his Jesus seeing Him face-to-face.

God has blessed me with the opportunity now to share time with some "more seasoned" folks, providing companion care. It's been an honor to also provide respite care for the parents of a now nine-year-old girl with autism. I've known her since her birth and love her like a granddaughter. Her loving, sweet personality brightens my days. Being autistic, her love for numbers prompts her to start conversations with strangers with, "How old are you?" Going to have her start asking, "Do you know Jesus?"

These days I worship at Forward Church of God. Once again, God has led me to where He wants me to be. Led by a very anointed man of God and his wife, many are healed, delivered, baptized, and receive the gifting of their prayer language. *"God is Spirit, and His worshippers must worship in the Spirit and in truth."* (John 4:24). God has been oh so faithful to me. *"I can see "the evidence of His goodness" all over my life… I see His promises in fulfillment,"* as Josh Baldwin sings. I'm excited to see what God has for me in the days to come. He has recently been using me once again to come alongside women in need, encouraging them in their spiritual and personal growth! I have just recently been chosen to be the house manager for a women's transitional house in Rock Hill, The Goshen House – and the next ministry adventure begins!

"Being confident of this very thing, that He which hath began a good work in you will perform it until the day of Jesus Christ." (Philippians 1:6). To God be all the glory! Amen!

I was born on November 26th, 1977, in Olympia, Washington. My father was a Captain in the U.S. Army and a Deputy Sheriff, and my mother was a Firefighter Paramedic. We lived in a small village called the Nisqually Valley at the base of Mount Rainier. We lived near my grandparent's farm, and I spent all my time there shadowing my grandfather, after whom I was named. For the most part, our family was closely knit, with large family gatherings at the farm for meals on the weekends and all the holidays. When I was in second grade, we moved to Alabama because my dad was stationed at Ft. McClellan for Military Police training - this was also the year my parents divorced. Shortly after dad finished training, he took off with my sister Rachael and me back to Washington. After a few years, I convinced my dad to allow me to go live with my mom in Alabama.

In the summer of 1990 after completing sixth grade, while visiting my dad for the summer, we took a family trip to a small mountain town in eastern Oregon. Life as I knew it was going to change forever. While rock climbing, we set out to find a place to repel. We found a spot about 150 feet up, and my dad had my sister and I sit back away from the drop point while my dad and stepmother set up. After what seemed like forever, my dad came running back to us, sweating and in a panic. He told my sister and me to get our things and let's go. When I asked him about my stepmother he said, "she'll meet us at the car." When we reached the entrance of the park where we left the car, I heard my stepmother yelling for help and saying, "don't leave me here, Randy!" I asked Dad what was going on and he told me to shut up and keep walking. When we got to the car, he did not once try to call for help just drove an hour back to our resort. Later that night, I was told my stepmother had died from her injuries.

The following fall Mom and I moved back to Washington. One day at school I was informed by my grandfather and a deputy that my dad had been arrested for murder. This would be a difficult school year. I changed schools twice, my sister moved in with us, and we had to return to Oregon several times for interviews, grand jury hearings, and ultimately his trial. Dad was found guilty of criminally negligent homicide and sentenced to five years in prison.

When this happened, my mom reunited with her high school sweetheart, and we were off to Tucson, Arizona. Mom married him shortly after moving there, and things felt like they were returning to normal. Then my stepdad started getting violent both physically and mentally with me. But I kept it hidden from my mom because she was happy – I was not. Two years later my stepdad's mother, sister, and sister's kids moved in with us, and six months later we all moved to Kentucky to be closer to his mother's family. By this time, I started to explore alcohol and benzos. I did this to numb the pain and block out the abuse. I'd drink and pop a pill when I couldn't take it anymore. It came to the point that I would take them to school just to get through the day.

During my junior year of high school, I enlisted in the Army Reserves through the split option program. This allowed me to go to basic training and return to finish my senior year before going to my training school. I also joined our town's volunteer fire department and received EMT training. I stopped popping pills and slowed down on my drinking because I did whatever I could to not be home whenever possible. While at basic training in Ft. Leonard-Wood, Missouri, I dislocated my shoulder so badly that they ended up discharging me medically because I didn't have enough time to heal and recirculate to the next training class and then be back in Kentucky in time for school. Feeling like a failure, I turned back to the booze. Before school started, I begged my mom to allow me to get married to my high school sweetheart. That marriage lasted a whole year before she filed for divorce because of my drinking. Then I quit school. I wrote some worthless checks to get my alcohol and to obtain things I wanted. Ol' Johnny Law finally caught up with me, and I ended up going in and out of the county jails for all the bad check charges - all misdemeanors. Probation, fines, and court costs were part of my life for the next few years.

I met the girl who would become my second wife in the fall of 1997, and I moved with her to her hometown in Illinois. I saw my mom for the first time in two years that Christmas. I was married in January, and she came to my reception, but soon my life took another drastic  step in the wrong direction. On February 20, 1998, I was notified that my stepdad had shot and killed my mom. Racing to get to her house, I found out my worst nightmare had come true. My mom was gone. During this difficult time, my wife told me I needed to stop crying and get over the fact that my mom was not coming back. I punched her and sent her packing back to Illinois, pregnant with my son. I was going through so much that I turned back to drinking heavily and went to live with my mom's sister in Arizona. I started to drink more frequently and heavily.

Realizing my son was going to be born without me, I moved back to Illinois, but I was living on the streets. Not long after my son was born, I moved back to Oregon and was living in a boarding house. I paid my bills and with whatever I had left over, I drank - and drank a lot. I met many different girls on the internet and moved from Colorado to South Carolina, Georgia, then Pennsylvania.

While in Pennsylvania, I was in a toxic relationship and didn't even realize it. When I was home, I was all about drinking, and when I was working, she was working too - as an escort. She gave birth to my son, and then a little girl. One morning after coming home from my shift, the sheriff's office came knocking on the door with a warrant for my girlfriend for felony credit card fraud and prostitution charges. The county Children and Youth Services took all the kids. So off to Michigan I went in search of true love, and then to Florida, then to Arizona, and back to Florida. Did I mention Texas? And South Carolina? As you can see, everywhere I went I took my problems with me. You can change your location but if you don't change you, nothing changes!

Another woman, then another baby - not what I wanted to hear. One night after coming home from work late at night, the babysitter told me that my wife was still at the bar, so she had stayed with the baby until I arrived home. Not long after she left to go home, my son woke up crying, so I picked him up and laid him on the bed to change him. When I was getting him a dry sleeper, I heard him choking and turned to see him choking on his vomit. I jerked him up trying to clear his airway and failed to hold his head to keep it from flopping around. He started to convulse, and he was turning blue. I was in panic mode. When the ambulance arrived, I gave my son to the medics, broke down in tears behind the ambulance, and started praying for the first time in a long time, begging God to save my son or take me instead. While at the hospital, they did a CT scan on my son and found a brain bleed. It was later determined that my failure to hold his head caused the bleeding while I was attempting to clear his airway.

DSS was called in to investigate and later charged me with unlawful conduct towards a child - a nasty way of saying felony child neglect. They stated that I should have acted differently in the situation because of my EMT training. I was arrested and sent to the Greenville County Detention Center. After Christmas and New Year's passed, I went up for a bond reduction and was released on my signature. I thought the charges had been dropped, and I attempted to get on with my life. I was wrong about the charges being dropped, and one day I came home to the SWAT team looking for me. Greenville County had me listed as a fugitive from justice and swore out a warrant for my arrest. I went peacefully and was extradited to South Carolina to answer for my mistakes. While I was in the county jail, my girlfriend left me; to this day, I have yet to meet my youngest daughter.

After about four months of going back and forth to court, I took a plea agreement to get this mess behind me. The deal was for a one-year active sentence and four years on probation. When I went in front of the judge, my ex stood up and painted a picture of how I abused my son. The judge then sentenced me to a ten-year suspended sentence, to serve five years non-

violent in the South Carolina Department of Corrections followed by three years of probation. My heart sank, and I dropped to my knees in tears. Is this where my life was going to end? I had never spent more than four months in the county jail, and now I would spend five years in prison, never to work as a paramedic again.

In July 2014, I arrived at Kirkland R&E and was processed as Inmate# 360560. While I was in Kirkland, I heard testimonies from others of how God can transform your life and how He can change your identity. I was thinking – if He could do this, why did He let all those bad things happen to me when I was a kid, and why did He allow my son to sustain the head injury? I was pretty angry with Him.

In September 2014, I was sent to Kershaw Correctional Institution. This is where I was going to spend my sentence as a level two, medium custody inmate. When I got off the bus and talked to the officer who was processing me into the institution he said, "you don't want to get mixed up with the gangs, and if I were you, I would look into getting into a program dorm. God does some great work here." The last thing I wanted to hear about was God, even though I was scared and alone with no family and no friends.

My first dorm was Palmetto B. I must have had a target on me because everyone could smell my fear. I went to my cell and met my roommate. He told me he was trying to get into the PTS (Prison To Society) program dorm. He explained that it was a character-based program offered by the chaplain to help inmates have a successful reentry back into society, but it was for short-timers. I had five years to serve, and there was no way I would qualify. Besides, you had to be a Christian, or so I thought. After I met with classification, I was informed that because I was a non-violent inmate, I would only have to do a portion of my time to max out. With time served, I was looking at maxing out in November of 2016. I was assigned to work in the kitchen, and one day coming back to the dorm, I was approached by MC. He was the TC (Transformation Church) small group leader for Palmetto. He invited me to sit in and check out the group. Figuring I had nothing to lose, I did. That's when I first heard Pastor Derwin Gray talk about God's amazing grace and perfect love. After the class ended, I asked MC more about this, and we talked for what seemed to be forever. He told me that I needed to speak with Chap (Chaplain Potoka) about PTS, saying that I didn't belong in Palmetto, so, I put in a request to see Chap.

At first, I was apprehensive about meeting a preacher. God hadn't been there for me before, so why now? But what did I have to lose, so I went to meet Chap. At first, I thought he was judgmental, just like every other Christian I had met. But I soon realized that wasn't the case, but he wouldn't let me play victim to my situation like I had done so many times. I filled out the religious paperwork and wrote Christian on it so I could go to church and get out of the dorm for an hour, even if it was for church. People started to pour positive things into my life: Chap, MC, and volunteers from TC church. I began to think there was something valuable to what they were planting inside of me. Eventually, I put in my application for PTS, was accepted, moved to Sycamore B, and started attending the required classes; I also signed up for a vocational training class.

I found myself going to church often, not just to get out of the dorm but because I was realizing that I was spiritually and emotionally hungry and lost. The next thing I knew, I was in the chapel's Sonlite

Choir. More people started to pour into my life, chipping away at my defensive and destructive walls. Even Chap was helping me change my perspective on life, and I stopped accepting that I was a victim of circumstances and began to take responsibility for the real reason I was in prison. I was even baptized! I joined AA to address my alcoholism, talked to mental health about my depression, and hesitated to take anything addictive from medical. Things were going great. Then my non-Christian roommate started to do something I didn't like, and we got into a heated argument, and I cussed him out, which was against the rules of PTS. I was set down from the choir, and Chap had mercy on me and allowed me to stay in PTS when he could have kicked me out.

Eventually, I got to a point in my sentence where I needed to get remedial classes and I started attending GED classes. This was the best thing I could do, not to mention it ended up being a stepping-stone for what was to come. I got back active with the choir and was notified that I was short enough on my sentence to join *SPICE*. This  was a more focused pre-release program for non-violent offenders who were paroled as a condition of their release, or those like me who simply wanted to change their future. I was moved to a *SPICE* room in the same dorm and took part in more focused, intensive classes - like Holistic Hardware, Employability, Consequences of Crime, and several Christian-based classes.

After graduating from *SPICE*, I only had six weeks left on my sentence. I had nowhere to go, and I couldn't leave South Carolina. Ms. Cook (the *SPICE* coordinator), Chap, and Sandy Perry (one of my instructors in PTS and *SPICE*) talked to me about the Zacchaeus House in Rock Hill (a transition house for men leaving prison). I applied and was accepted into their program, and Sandy, the house director, helped me transfer my probation from Greenville County to York County. On November 1st, 2016, I was released from prison to restart my life. It was scary getting back into society. For the past two and a half years, I had my days planned out for me, and it was what I had become accustomed to. I hadn't been good at making good choices in the past, but Sandy and Vicki had everything in place to ease my transition from prison to society - the only thing I had an issue with was the rule of no female relationships.

I met Amber 18 days after my release. We had to sneak to see each other, but eventually, we were found out and we had to stop dating, or I would be kicked out of the program. I was outraged, but I couldn't risk losing my bed, so Amber and I agreed it was for the best - even if it sucked. We talked every day and night via phone and text. Then in April 2017, when my six months at Zacchaeus House were up, I moved out and in with her; we were married that August. I was promoted to a team lead position at Tractor Supply Company where I worked. I also enrolled in business school at Ohio Christian University - in September 2017 I was officially hired as a Team Lead/ Key Holder for Tractor Supply. God was showing Himself faithful to me.

ASSOCIATE ARTS

From there, I worked many different jobs, each making more money than the last until I landed a manager's position with the company I am with now. After graduating with my Associate in Arts with a major in Business Management, I was promoted to Operations Manager and given a substantial raise in pay. Since then, we have bought two cars and a house, go to church every chance we get, and I serve as an usher and a member of the prison ministry team. Am I a misfit? By all definitions, yes! But my past is my testimony of God's perfect love and grace, and my future is brighter than ever!

JAMES

Throughout my life, I have suffered from poor decision-making. Ultimately, my own bad choices have brought me back to prison again. I have tried to pinpoint a particular situation and say, "that's what brought me back to prison," but I can't. Somehow, I had lost my way. My life's focus was no longer about Christ – it was all about me!

 In June 2009, I was released from prison and immediately went to work on the goals I had set for myself while incarcerated. My goals were put in place on the first day of my release and continued until the fifth year of freedom. Every goal had a specific action attached to ensure its accomplishment. Most of these goals were accomplished with little difficulty. Some I had done before so I was aware of what I would have to endure. Others would take a little more tenacity.

While I would love to tell you that I completed all these goals and set even higher and greater goals as well, that just didn't happen. Why? Because I was a quitter! Every time something got challenging or difficult, I'd quit. I had a quitter mindset. Usually, when I'd see someone quit something I would say, "cool, try something else. That might not be what you are supposed to be doing." But anything worth having doesn't come easy. The things that I quit pursuing in life were all worth having, but I always found myself giving up. Recently I asked myself why I always seem to fail at the things I most want to be successful at.

I started doing that a few years ago - asking myself serious questions, not so much about what I was doing, but why. I began journaling when I was in conversations with other people and helpful suggestions jumped out at me that seemed helpful. But one problem was that I was wearing vulnerability like a garment – I discovered that I was too easily wounded.

I believe I was damaged emotionally in my younger years. I was exposed to many things that were done, and said, or were never said at all and should have been. In many ways, my family seemed normal, but we were far from being a healthy functional unit. Mom & Dad divorced when I was six or seven – their relationship was toxic, which made my siblings and me suffer through drunken arguments and fights. When Dad left, Mom had full responsibility for raising four children, and when she turned to alcohol, she quit being a mother. By the time she and my dad made any meaningful attempts to correct mistakes they had made, I had already turned to my older brother as my role model. I made up my mind that I was going to do whatever pleased me – that's what eventually led to my first incarceration. I never became the physical abuser that my father was, but there were other harmful things I did learn from him; one being promiscuity. Being faithful to one woman wasn't in my blood. It was not a concept that I wanted or even understood. So, every time a relationship with a woman got to the expectation of commitment, I would run to another woman. It seemed less complicated doing things Dad's way.

This dysfunction has followed me into adulthood and infected my attitude, feelings, and behaviors. The quitter mindset. Why should I bother? Why should I care? What difference does it make? So, I walked away from some great opportunities that I should have taken advantage of, and I made one bad decision after another. Does it really matter anyway?

One of the goals I had set for myself when I was released from prison was to faithfully attend church. Things were going so well for me when I hit the streets: job, transportation, girlfriend, and a restored relationship with my son – God was being so good to me, but I neglected my plan of going to church. Was it that I was ungrateful? Not really. I just didn't see the urgency. Don't most people run to church when they have needs? I didn't, maybe because I was too comfortable with how wonderful God was performing in my life.

I finally did start attending church about a year after I got home. I joined the required 15-week membership class that was a prerequisite for getting involved in the church's ministry teams. I wanted to help people who needed material goods and services, as well as support and encouragement, so each lesson spoke to my heart in a meaningful way, preparing me for church ministry. By the end of the 15 weeks, I was excited and ready to do ministry, and my heart leaped at the thought of doing prison ministry through the church.

I started a cleaning business as soon as I left prison, and since our church was preparing to move to a larger campus (an older shopping mall that was being converted into a church), I stopped by the new site as construction was being completed. The pastor indicated he wanted to talk to me about my company giving them a quote on cleaning all the windows in the renovated building. I was glad to help and happy for the work. When I submitted my estimate to the church, I was told, "we have a guy that gave us a cheaper price. I

think he's a crackhead." Once again, I wanted to quit. The enemy had me in his crosshairs once more hammering me with discouragement, frustration, and defeat. While it might be true that Crackhead Freddie needed work - so did I. I also needed their support! I was only out of prison one year and struggling to be independent and self-reliant - and I wasn't on drugs. So, I just quit. Again.

Once the new campus was up and running, I started attending again, every Sunday and Wednesday. I put the disappointment behind me and became a valued church member. I even paid my tithes and gave freewill offerings, and God continued to bless every area of my life, but I still wanted to go back inside the prison and try to make a difference in the lives of other men. Then one day I got a call from the South Carolina HIV/AIDS Council (SCHAC) where I worked while at Campbell Work-Release, and then when released from SCDC. They asked if I would help to facilitate a training program called, *Pharoah*. This health initiative is an HIV/safe sex intervention designed by the Baltimore Health Department for heterosexual males who were HIV-negative.

I jumped at the opportunity to teach these classes once again at homeless shelters and correctional facilities. We had invitations to go into Broad River, Evans, and Turbeville prisons in hopes that the program participants would learn, and then teach others about HIV preventive methods. It was my hope that this opportunity would help open more doors for future prison ministry – but all that I hoped for never materialized, feeding my quitter mindset. Everything fell apart, and James retreated once again.

Again, I thought I had the opportunity at my church to join their prison ministry team, currently consisting only of one deacon. He partnered with other churches since he was working alone, so on several occasions I extended an offer to join him, but it fell on deaf

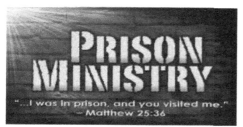

ears. Not long after that, I left that church. The *Pharoah* program was now going well – going back into the prisons to serve was a big moment for me. But shortly thereafter, the Warden at Broad River said I could no longer come in there because I was "gang affiliated." Another blow to my already fragile mindset. I had one focus for giving back - prison ministry; and if I could no longer do that, I no longer wanted to do anything else. There were other smaller churches that I could have gone to and gotten involved there – but I didn't.

I had a cleaning contract with Columbia International University to annually perform some pressure washing and window cleaning in preparation for the new school term. The facilities manager and I had become close, so when a full-time janitorial position came at their high school campus (including medical benefits and tuition discounts for the university), he wanted to hire me - I declined his offer.

There was a volunteer where I was incarcerated, fondly called *Boxcar Willie*, who taught an *Alpha* class titled: *Choices*. Today, I am sitting once again in the same dorm (in the same prison) 13 years later reflecting on the choices that I made that brought me back to prison – a series of bad decisions, one mistake after another. It was when I decided to leave that church that my life began to fall apart. I began to think the world was against me. I was making decisions based on my feelings, instead of what was the right thing, or the wise thing to do.

Romans chapter 12 in the Bible admonishes us as believers to offer ourselves as a living sacrifice to God for His service, and don't be conformed to what the world around us is doing, but to be transformed by the renewing of our minds. God has opened to me many doors of opportunity to serve Him by ministering to other people, but I closed them all, not considering what would have been pleasing to the One who died for me. What if I had never been a quitter? That is water under the bridge now – my new plan is to begin renewing my mind with God's Word and living in joyful obedience to Him.

NATION
of
ISLAM

I grew up in the Bronx, NY. I didn't grow up attending church – we attended the Mosque as members of the Nation of Islam. As a family, we were serious about our beliefs. My two brothers were even members of the FOI (Fighters of Islam). But when I was about six years old, Elijah Muhammad died, and we stopped attending services. This was primarily due to the Nation of Islam not agreeing on who should take over the Nation's spiritual leadership. Louis Farrakhan eventually became the recognized leader, but it caused major issues for some followers because many expected Elijah Muhammad's biological son to assume the role of leader.

At home, the household was one of constant dysfunction and abuse. My parents were tough on me, which I now appreciate, but still, I pretty much got whatever I wanted. They were both in their 40s when I came along, so I grew up living like I was being raised by my grandparents - and you know how grandparents are! I remember growing up having a lot of fun - maybe too much fun. That was my main goal in life, so I thought everything else was okay. Too much fun and too little moral supervision – trouble was brewing!

I was still in elementary school when I was first introduced to porn. My dad was a huge porn fan and although he kept his collections locked up, I figured out a way to get to them. My first experience with porn came in the form of magazines. There were lots of magazines that captured the attention of an impressionable schoolboy. Next was VHS tapes, and when the internet came along, I was on it. All the porn an undisciplined boy could want. Once, my mother found my stash under the mattress and told my dad. His response was amazing for me at the time. I thought I was going to be in trouble, but his response was simply, "He's a boy - He'll be all right". That was the green light for me for the next few years as far as I was concerned. But little supervision resulted in big trouble in my life.

Everything changed when I met a young lady in the summer between my freshman and sophomore years of high school. All that I had seen in magazines and watched on the internet went from fantasy to real flesh. My habits and my addiction began impacting another person. When my mother found out and told my dad, his response was what I wanted, but not what I needed to hear. "He's no faggot" was his ringing endorsement of the lifestyle I was living. You see, growing up I wanted my dad's approval, no matter whether it was for good or bad behavior. I just wanted his approval of me as his son. Two thumbs up from him said I was a great son, or so I thought. My porn addiction continued for many, many years. In fact, porn ruled my life from 1982 through 2015. I was heavily addicted and becoming heavily damaged.

During that same time in my life, another bad habit was developing into another addiction - cocaine. Coke. Blow. Nose candy? I started sniffing it when I was 17-18 years old, and I fell in love with it. It made me feel like I was on top of the world. My friends would call me snowman because I always kept it on me - some to use and some to sell. Weed first, cocaine next, and then selling (but not using) crack. I never made a lot of money because I was often my own best customer, sniffing up my nose all the profits I had made. This habit/addiction lasted until my daughter was about two years old. I had a dream one night that my wife had learned about my addiction and threatened to leave me and take my daughter. The thought of that was enough for me to give it up altogether.

Religion was way off my radar during this time, although I do remember one time my wife wrote a note and placed it on the mirror in the bathroom. I didn't pay attention to it at first, because she would often write all types of crazy religious stuff, but this time I saw my name. So, I decided to read it. How shocking it was when I read, "Jamal is a blood-bought, fire-baptized Christian". What??? That was it - the whole note. Why was I, a nominal Muslim at the time, being called a Christian? That was worse than cursing me out. In anger, I lost my composure. I balled it up and threw it in her face after cussing her out. But 1998 would turn out to be a life-changing year for me. Soon after this incident, I found myself going to church, but only to shut her up. But something different happened in October of that year. I felt something funny inside, like a warm lightbulb over my head; close enough to feel the warmth but far enough to not burn me. At that time, I wasn't familiar with anything in Christianity so I really couldn't explain what was behind it. I asked a few people that I trusted if they knew what this was, and they told me it was the Holy Spirit resting on me. I went with it even though I didn't know anything about what they were saying, but it sounded good.

Eventually, I began to attend church more often. Soon, it was every Sunday. I even started going to Wednesday night Bible study. It was fun and it was fashionable, but I didn't really know what I was doing;

it was for show. The pastor introduced me to the Lord via basketball and he included me when planning youth events – he knew I loved working with youth. Then I was baptized. Me a baptized Christian? I had spent so many days in the park or at school tearing Christians down, telling them they were stupid. Especially black people! Jesus was always depicted as this white guy with blue eyes and blonde hair; a European metrosexual hair shampoo model - the very thing I had been taught to hate as a child. Remember, I grew up in the Nation of Islam. How could I now start worshipping Jesus?

I decide to live my new life as a Christian on the low, meaning I wasn't eager to share it with anyone, especially my family back in NYC, although they were no longer attending the Mosque. Some were even going to church now, but we still had our belief along the lines of the Nation of Islam. No pork, but also no doctrine. I was not saying grace over the food at mealtimes or mentioning any other Christian beliefs or lifestyle choices. But I was trying to do good to my family, do good to others, and be an all-around good person. But absolutely no mention of Jesus Christ. Ever!

Some years passed, and I was doing more than just attending. I started to get more involved with the church. I even got baptized, this time for real. I began serving in the church in various roles but leading the youth ministry was the most impactful – for the youth, and for me. I began to teach Wednesday night teen Bible study, then started helping in children's church on Sundays. It was great, I finally felt I was doing "the right thing" - but I was serving two gods.

In 2009, I moved my family to Charlotte, NC. It wasn't long after arriving there that I found myself divorced and a single dad. It was a struggle trying to work on second shift and be a good father too. Eventually, my daughter moved in with my ex-wife and it was just my son and me from early 2011 until 2014. I went out on a few dates here and there but nothing serious at all. I had been praying for God to bring that someone special into my life. I didn't want to date anymore, I wanted to be married. And one day there she was, at church! After several months of seeing her, I finally gathered enough courage to ask her out and a few months later to marry me. After being married for 7-8 months, my dark habit revealed its ugly head, and she knew I had been looking at porn regularly. We separated for about a week and I promised her I would not look at porn anymore. I joined a group and sought out counseling for my addiction. It was hard but I know I had to change for my wife. There was the problem - I did it for my wife, not for God.

It wasn't long before I started placing my wife on a pedestal. She became more important than anything, even God Himself. I began to praise her, and worship her and I had such high esteem for her, but not of her. That failed expectation eventually gave way to me stepping out and cheating on her. A year went by before she found out, but the marriage had taken a major blow at this point. We separated and I was to blame. My family was gone. I headed straight to church and requested to see someone about my issues and the burning desire to have my wife back. I met with Pastor Ken, one of the pastors at our church. Ken sat me down and gave me the hard, real truth about my behaviors and the real possibility that my marriage may be gone for good. There was another brother in Christ at the church as well, Larry. For the first time in my life, I can say I had real Christian mentors to help guide me on this uphill walk. They called me out and broke me down and held my feet to the fire. And they loved me back to health - physical and spiritual health. I joined a small, intimate men's group addressing many of the issues, habits, and problems I had faced from childhood, and they held me accountable for my choices.

What is a true Christian?

The most important thing I found out during this time was that I wasn't a true Christian. I had just been a religious actor. And I was a superb actor. I had done everything just right, at least what people could see, but I had deep, dark secrets. I had wanted to identify with Christ but had never surrendered my life or submitted my will to Jesus. Pastor Ken opened my eyes when he explained to me a crucial mistake that I was making. I told him I had been praying for years to be a father like God and a husband like Jesus. He suggested that I needed to focus on being God's son and being the best son that I could be. I accepted the challenge and decided that I was going to be the best son God ever had, outside of Jesus. If my wife and I were to get back together, God is great. But if we were never to get back together, God is still great; either way, God is great, and I would strive to be His faithful son. On October 8, 2017, I was baptized. This time it truly was an outward sign that I had spiritually died to my sin and to my own self, and I was raised up to live a new life in Christ. I was finally fully surrendered, and fully submitted to God's will for my life. By the grace of God, and the encouragement of godly men in my life, I have never again cheated on my wife, I haven't looked at porn in over seven years, and I am still learning how to be God's adopted son. I look forward every day to fulfilling God's desire for my life.

Currently, I am serving in my church, running a new men's shelter and transition home through Tender Hearts Ministry in York, SC, and serving in missions in Greece. I am a Misfit, but I am also a Miracle!

I was laying in the back of the car trying to sleep over the sound of AC/DC blasting and my mom and dad screaming at each other. Being thrown from side to side as my dad took the curves at high speed made sleep even more difficult. I couldn't have been more than five years old. Nights like this came often, and it didn't matter how much I screamed for them to stop fighting, they wouldn't. So, I just cried silently to myself until the car stopped or I would finally fall asleep.

My dad had a big family, and I grew up with lots of cousins to play with. Grandma's house was the place to be because that's where we lived and that's where the family would gather. Uncle Billy and his wife, Candy, also lived there. Along with the family ties, they also had strong ties to alcohol. One fall morning I was getting ready for school, and we had a knock on the door. My grandma let out the most blood-curdling scream one could imagine. It was the police with news that Uncle Billy and my dad had been in a terrible car accident. They needed my grandparents to go identify a body. Uncle Billy had died, and Dad had been flown to Baptist Hospital in critical condition. He ended up surviving, but his left leg was amputated, along with other severe injuries.

After months of rehab and learning to walk again, my parents decided it was time to move away from the rest of the family and start fresh. We moved to where my father was born and raised in West Virginia; I was seven years old. The settlement daddy received from the crash was enough for us to buy a home but moving away from the family didn't mean the drinking would stop. One day my brother and I were sitting on the living room floor playing while Dad watched TV. He fell to his knees, screaming for my mom while holding his chest. This was the first time I had ever heard my daddy pray. I learned later he thought he was having a heart attack, but something changed about him that day. My parents poured all the alcohol down the sink, and we started going to church.

My mother was never very close with her family, but her grandparents lived in the same town as us. He was a Baptist pastor and we used to listen to him preach on the radio on Sundays. She would always tell me with such pride in her voice, "that's Pop-paw on the radio." Since he was a pastor, and my parents were ready to attend church it made sense that we would go to the church where he preached. This was the beginning of the good days. Daddy started reading the Bible  to my brother and me. He even had an old hymn book that we would sing, *Victory in Jesus* and *I'll Fly Away*. My great-grandparents loved Jesus and told me all about Him. Life was good for a few years: my parents were not fighting as often, there was no alcohol, and we were spending time with people who loved the Lord. Things took a turn for the worse when my mom's mother died. Mom started back drinking - heavy. Dad was having trouble finding work in WV, so he decided to go back to NC and stay with my grandparents through the week for work, and he would come back home on weekends. The plan was to eventually sell the house and move back to NC.

I was 12 years old, and my daddy was in NC working. My brother and I were in school, but that didn't seem to matter much to my mom because she would keep us out all hours of the night. Some nights we never made it home, or to school the next day. My grandfather's half-brother had several children, and they were all around my mom's age. Most nights they would all just listen to loud music and drink; until it became more than that. I walked into the kitchen where she sat with the oldest brother, kissing. I remember crying and asking her why she was kissing him. I was so upset and the first thing I planned to do was call my daddy. By this time, the youngest brother, who was 20 years old, had begun showing me "special attention." He and my mom tried to explain how much trouble it would cause if I told my dad. They told me I couldn't tell, because someone could die, and it might be my dad. So, the fear of losing my dad, to death or prison, forced me to keep the secret. Every weekend my dad would come home, and I would watch my mom act as if nothing was happening. The secret I was keeping caused me to hate her.

I felt so alone. I didn't have my dad around and my mom seemed to care more about her new boyfriend - and liquor. The youngest brother, whom we will call, Scott, seemed to be the only person in the world who cared about me. I felt that he was the only person in my life who didn't dismiss my feelings or discredit me as a child. I told him about my plan to tell my dad because keeping the secret felt like I was betraying him just like my mom was. That night, my mom called me out to the porch to tell me that she noticed how much I liked Scott and how much time I was spending with him. She told me he liked me too, but he liked me more than a friend. Momma told me I was old enough to have a boyfriend, but I couldn't tell my dad that we both had boyfriends. Then we went back into the house where she told Scott that it was ok for him to be my boyfriend, but no one could know. He had made several remarks to me before that night about how  my breasts were growing or how my clothes fit, but he had never touched me before she gave him the approval. The secrets were tearing me apart. My dad knew something was wrong, but there was no way I could tell him about momma now because I had been warned several times that if I told her secret, she would tell mine. Shame and guilt were my two new best friends. I could no longer stand my mother. The worst thing in the world was watching her kiss my daddy on the weekends after seeing her hugged up with another man all week.

Apparently, my mom got a guilty conscience, because one night they went to a bar while my dad was home, and she told him she had been seeing someone else and wanted a divorce. The next thing I knew my dad was throwing all her things into the front yard. I didn't realize she hadn't told him that she was allowing his 12-year-old daughter to have a 20-year-old boyfriend. The details of what followed were horrific, but I will save those for another time. After finding out all that was happening to me, my dad decided to press charges against Scott. I remember going to the police station to be interviewed. They asked where my mother was when this was happening, and I told them she knew about it and was there. She was arrested as well. She called my dad from jail begging him to get her out. He fell for it and bonded her out the same day. I was told that if I didn't tell the police I was lying about my mom, she would go to prison, and I would not see her for a very long time. Again, the fear of losing a parent to prison forced me to keep another secret and tell the police I had told them a lie. They dropped the charges on her.

Scott was in jail for a while, but when he was released on bond he came to my house in the middle of the night and begged me to go for a ride with him to talk. I did, but that ride lasted eight days. He kept me hostage in the woods before stealing a car to take me to Florida. On our way, we were in a high-speed police chase that ended with us crashing on the interstate. He was arrested and I was taken to the police station to wait on my parents. I sat in the police station all night, feeling completely abandoned as I waited on them.

Once I was back home my parents didn't know what to do with me. So, they decided to medicate me with marijuana. It worked for them, surely it would help me. At 13, I was smoking weed every day. I was full of rage, shame, and guilt and I wanted to die. I ended up in the psych ward for the first time where once again, I learned that adults  couldn't be trusted when one of the psych techs molested me. Just another secret I had to keep because no one would believe "the little whore" anyway. That was my new name. I was first called that by my father the night he found out about everything with Scott.

I began to live up to my new name and was very promiscuous. Attention from boys fed that longing to be noticed by someone - anyone. When I was 14, I got noticed by my aunt's husband. That was certainly unwanted attention, but he told me he would kill my family if I told anyone what he made me do to pleasure him. I believed it because he was part of the Hell's Angels and stories were floating around about how he had killed people. Three years later he killed my aunt and threw her body along the highway. He never did any prison time for what he did to me, but he did go to prison for her murder.

Another visit to the psych ward occurred when I was 16. I slit my wrists, but it was mostly for attention. I guess it was a cry for help, really. I just wanted someone to see my pain - to see how unwanted and unloved I felt. I remembered singing the songs about Jesus, and I remembered hearing them preach about Him, but He seemed to have forgotten me. I wondered if He was even God. I mean, how could I be sure? How arrogant did Christians have to be to believe that there could only be one true God - Jesus?

At 17, I decided to do a new drug for the first time. I fell in love with it and the second chance I had to do it again came through a man that worked in a nail salon. He offered it to me if my friend and I would go clubbing with him. Of course, we couldn't pass up the opportunity to get free fake IDs, drugs, and a trip to the club. We went, but I never imagined that I would come face to face with Satan that night. Standing in the parking lot of a building they called "the club," my body completely froze. I felt like I was dying and as I looked around, I saw into the spiritual realm. Yes, I was on the drug at this time, but there is no doubt in my mind that I was surrounded by demons. I saw them, and I knew I was dying and going to hell. At that very moment, God spoke to me and told me to choose life or death. I  chose life, and I screamed for my friend to come back to the car. I don't share that part of my story often because I'm sure I was in a

drug-induced state of psychosis, but whatever it was it definitely got my attention.

By the age of 19, I was pregnant and married to my first husband who was my high-school sweetheart. He didn't understand this change that had taken place in me and why I was so obsessed with Jesus. He still wanted to party, and I wanted to raise my child different from the way I had grown up. The marriage didn't last long, so now I found myself being a single mom. Here I was again, alone, this time with another human to care for. In my despair, I started hanging around old friends again. I was the youngest one in my church and the only single mom. These church people couldn't relate to me. It wasn't long before I gave up going to church altogether and started using pills to get through the day. The next eight years of my life would be a living hell.

I began a relationship with an alcoholic who was mentally and physically abusive. After having his child, I found it even harder to leave him. I would do good for a short time; get a job, and have my own place, but then let him move back in and lose it all – again! My drug use spiraled out of control, and I was drinking more than ever. After another suicide attempt, I landed back in the psych ward where I met a girl that swore Jesus had come to her in a dream and said she was supposed to help me. She even got her mother involved. Her mom found this place in Charlotte, NC, called El Roi Ministries. This was a home for girls who had a history of sexual abuse. This was where I met the most Christ-loving people I have ever known, and they loved me too!

I moved into their home with other girls who were like me in a lot of ways. We went to church and had Bible study throughout the week. I watched this couple's every move, waiting on them to hurt me in some way like all the people from my past. I watched how they interacted with one another, how much they loved each other, and literally every person they encountered. Gerry (Pop) and Eileen (Mom) Potoka were not like anyone I had ever met. They lived out what they said they believed. I remember wishing that I had been born as their daughter. Then, they started calling me their daughter, and that was the greatest compliment I had ever received. Someone like me could actually be given such an honor? What I now know about being a godly woman and wife I learned from Eileen. Pop taught me how a man is supposed to treat a woman, and practical ways to apply scripture to my life. He taught me that God was not only just, but He was kind, loving, and merciful. It didn't matter what I had done or where I had been, Jesus still wanted a relationship with me, and He gave His life so that I could stand before God justified.

I wish I could say that I turned to Christ during that time, but I didn't. I lived with them for about a year before going back to my old life. During that time, they became house parents of a maternity home, and I stayed in one of the aftercare homes across the street. God had a plan! But unfortunately, I had my own plan. I still had that relationship with my son's father that pulled me back to self-destruction every time.

I moved back to Statesville, my old stomping ground, and my life took a fast turn for the worse - again. I went from one drug to the other. I became homeless and everything I owned fit in three trash bags. I lost my children, I was hopeless, lost, and broken. I didn't even feel worthy to be called a mother. I thought it was best that my children were with their dads' families. Drugs had consumed me, and I thought I would die in the streets. From time to time, I would call Pop. I think I just wanted to see if he still loved me and would answer the phone. He always answered, and he always told me he loved me. When he told me he loved me, I believed it. When other people used those words, they were just empty words because their actions always proved different. At my lowest point, I could always call Pop and he would answer. Quite honestly, I didn't have anyone else to call.

 I ended up with a warrant for my arrest for a failure to appear in court. I was facing three years in prison for two DUIs and drug paraphernalia charges. By this time, I was pregnant with my third child by my drug dealer. I couldn't go to

prison pregnant, and I couldn't have another child I couldn't take care of. I wanted to take care of this situation before I turned myself in. I called an abortion clinic and made an appointment, even though I never believed in abortion. I just couldn't see any other way out of this. I couldn't have a baby with this man. He had lots of other kids and took care of none of them. Before I made it to the abortion clinic I was arrested again. While I was in jail, I was happy to be in a place where I could shower and eat. At least I knew my baby was getting fed. I prayed on my first night there that God would change my life or kill me. I couldn't go on living this way.

I started reading the Bible every day and praying. There was a lady who came to lead Bible studies in the jail, and I attended each one. I was facing three years, but I had honestly come to a place where I felt peace about it. I decided that in prison or out of prison, I was going to live for Jesus. My lawyer came one day to tell me the jail was releasing me. He had gotten the sentence dropped to probation. By this time, I was too far along to abort. I still knew that I couldn't have another baby. I remembered the maternity home, so I called and was admitted to their program.

Once I moved into Lois' Lodge, I met with an adoption counselor. It was the hardest choice I have ever made, but it was the best choice for my son. I wanted him to have two parents who could provide everything he needed. I could barely provide for the two boys I already had, let alone another child. I saw the pain in my boys from their fathers not being what they needed. I couldn't bear seeing another child go through that type of pain. By choosing adoption, I gave this son everything I ever wanted for him. I prayed daily that God would choose the perfect family because I knew if he chose them my child would be where he was supposed to be. God did just that.

When one is entering into an adoption plan, the agency will give you several family portfolios to look through before making your choice of which family you want for your child. I looked at one, and I immediately felt a connection with that family and chose them. The family was on their way to the hospital, and I was battling my own fears, feelings of failure, and selfishness. I did not want another woman raising the son I just gave birth to. I had the opportunity to be alone with him for the first day after his birth, as the family was still in transit to my state. I took one look at this beautiful baby boy, and I knew that my life would never be the same. He was so tiny and perfect in every way. I picked him up and whispered softly, "thank you for saving my life. I promise I will be different when you come back to me one day." That promise to my son was my motivation from that day forward. I would never go back to the streets. I would never again let drugs rule my life. I truly believed that one day we would be reunited, and I wanted him to be proud of the woman he met. Being that the adoption was open, I knew that the family would send pictures and letters. I wanted to have an address to receive them - I couldn't be homeless ever again.

 The family arrived and I remember feeling so shameful. As I sat with the mom, I couldn't stop comparing myself to her. She had a college degree, a beautiful family, and a husband who loved her. She was smart and confident. I was a broken mess with nothing to show for my life. Three children by three different men, a high-school drop-out, no home, and my other children were not even living with me. In my mind, she was probably judging me like most other people in my life. She never said anything to lead me to believe that she thought she was better than me, but she didn't have to - I believed she was better than me.

I chose the name Ezekiel for my son, but the adoption agency told me that the family could change his name to whatever they decided. His new mom sat by my hospital bed, and we discussed his name. She had a paper that she and her husband had scribbled some names the moment they received the call that they had a son. With tears streaming down her face, she told me that Ezekiel was the first name they had chosen, even before finding out that was the same name I had picked for him. Ezekiel means, "strength of God." What a fitting name for this child because that's exactly what it took for me to move forward with the adoption. From that moment, I had no doubt in my mind that God had chosen this family for Zeke.

I was released from the hospital before Ezekiel was born but was able to visit every day while he was still in the neonatal unit. My other two boys were able to visit their brother and navigating their emotions around the adoption added another layer of pain to their situation. We spent time with Zeke's new family, and his mom even wanted me to go shopping with her to pick some things out for Zeke. The more I spent time with her, the more I realized how much she truly accepted me. Satan will use the lies you believe about yourself to make you think the whole world is against you.

Mom and Pop were also a part of my life during this time. Although I had given them much grief while I lived with them (a story for another time), Mom decided she would like to be my mentor when I entered the maternity home. She was also by my bedside at the hospital when Zeke was born. Her support and prayers carried me through. Not to mention, she never cared more about my feelings than telling me what I needed to hear. I loved her for that.

After they took Zeke back home, I went through an extended time of agonizing grief. I felt like a piece of my heart had been taken. I had moved into a drug treatment facility from the maternity home before he was born - God's sovereign hand over my life. If I had been on my own, it may have been too much to bear. The in-patient treatment placed me in an environment where I could process what I was experiencing in a safe environment. Not only did I need to process the adoption, but I also needed to deal with the trauma that led to my using drugs. Group therapy, NA meetings, individual counseling, random drug screenings, and a sponsor through NA that I met with regularly - that was my life for the next two years.

My friends from NA understood my struggles when I wanted to use, and they called me out when I was trying to rationalize and justify myself. They knew the addicts' games and saw through my manipulation. I needed these people, and they helped me stay clean. I shared some of my darkest secrets with them because I didn't feel judged. They had done the same things I had done for drugs, or worse. My counselors helped me dig deep to understand the "why" behind my constant need to escape the reality of my life. I was able to make connections and see unhealthy patterns, while also identifying the lies I believed about myself.

I also attended church and God placed a wonderful group of people around me who constantly led me back to His Word on days when I felt like I couldn't continue. For the first time in my life, I had an army of support around me. My church family was full of grace and love. When I needed anything, they were there. They drove me back and forth to pick up my children for visits. In the first year of my stay at the treatment facility, one of my sons came to live with me permanently. Getting my oldest back would take time, but my church family made sure I was able to see him regularly. I didn't have a car, so I couldn't drive the 60+ miles to pick him up unless I had a ride. The Lord gifted me with people who were willing to fight with me through the hard times. When I graduated from the program, these same people joined together and furnished my entire apartment. It was the greatest reminder of God's love for me.

Your Relationship With God Is The Best One You Will Ever Have

My relationship with the Lord continued to grow. I would spend hours studying His Word and praying. My life was now His to use however He desired. The longer I walked with Him, the more I hungered to know Him. He gradually changed my heart so that I no longer needed or desired my past life. My only desire was to please Him. I knew long ago that God had a plan for my life. I just never imagined that He could use the filthiest, vilest details of my story to help someone else. The things that brought me shame were the same things that gave others hope for a better way. This realization began in the rooms of Narcotics Anonymous. I started to see glimmers of hope in the eyes of other women who were only a few days clean when I would share my story. God was teaching me that everything the enemy meant for evil, He was using it for good. I joined with other ministry opportunities to serve the broken, which included jail and prison ministry. Since Pop was the chaplain of a prison, I was able to speak to the inmates and share how God had transformed my life.

I decided to go to college. Although I dropped out of high school, I managed to get my GED. I enrolled in the Human Services program with plans to be a substance abuse counselor. In my third semester of the program, the thought came to me that I was spending so much time studying secular approaches to addressing the dysfunction in the lives of others, but what I was really passionate about was how Jesus could address the dysfunction. One thing I noticed in the rooms of NA is that while people were staying clean, they were still engaging in all types of other sinful behaviors. Even those who had been clean for 20 years were still jumping from man to man or using people in other ways. Narcotics Anonymous certainly addresses the issue of drug use, but it doesn't have the power to free the soul from the bondage of sin. Only Jesus can do that, and people needed to know true freedom through Him. So, I left the Human Services program and enrolled in seminary.

During this time, God saw fit to bless me with a husband. It was only after I became emotionally healthy and whole in who I was in Christ that this man came into my life. Jamal is not perfect, but he is certainly God's chosen man for me. He loves me despite my flaws, and we pursue Christ together. We have now been married for eight years. He is a father to my boys, who have both lived with us for the past seven years. He is a good provider and protector; unlike any other man I had been with in the past. I couldn't ask for a better life than the one I live today. We now own our own home and Jamal is in full-time ministry serving as the director at a homeless

shelter for men. By God's grace, I am now the Executive Director of a pregnancy center where I have the opportunity to share Zeke's story daily.

Throughout my own struggle with drugs and alcohol, God gave me grace and empathy for my parents. My parents were addicts, and addicts always put themselves first. Realizing the great debt that was paid so that I could be forgiven made me capable of forgiving my parents. I love my mom and dad. Although they did harm to me, they also taught me lessons that I couldn't have learned any other way. My life as a child wasn't always a horror story. There were happy times when we went on family vacations, laughed a lot, and loved one another. I have prayed every day since surrendering my life to Christ that my mom, dad, and brother would also be saved and experience God's mercy. Two years ago, my father moved from WV to live with us. He started attending church and he has been going ever since. He finally moved into his own house this year, and my brother moved from Colorado to live with him. He is also attending church with us now. God is working in my family - a family of true misfits!

My story is not unique. There are thousands of people with stories like mine. People who have lived detestable lives but are completely transformed and made new in Christ. My hope for anyone reading this is that you might know that He is the one true God, the one who came to us because we can do nothing to make ourselves worthy to go to Him. He came to rescue us so we could stand before Him guiltless. Your story doesn't have to be like mine for you to need a Savior. ALL are guilty of offending our holy God. I'm so thankful that our sin doesn't have to end with eternal separation from God. Exodus 34:7 states that He (God) "cannot leave the guilty

unpunished." If God is just, and He is, there must be a consequence, a payment for sin – the wages of sin is death! Justice demands that God does not leave the guilty unpunished. Love is what drove Jesus to the cross in our place. God sent Jesus to take the punishment due us so that we could be free from condemnation. Our response is simply understanding that our sin has separated us from Him, turning away from that sin, and trusting in the work of Jesus on the cross on our behalf.

Just before Jesus took his last breath on the cross, He uttered the words, "It is finished" (John 19:30). The bondage of sin was broken at that moment for anyone who seeks life in Him. If you are like me, it may be hard to receive the gift Jesus has given. Maybe you feel unworthy like I did. Spoiler alert - you are! And I am as well! Jesus has something better for you, just like He did for me. When I truly understood that His way was best and that nothing in this world could satisfy the emptiness I felt in my heart, I became willing to do whatever He asked of me, and he became my Lord.

Psalm 23:3 says, "He restores my soul; He leads me on paths of righteousness for His name's sake." Any misfit that desires to be rescued and restored can receive that righteousness. Your life can be a reflection of His goodness and love. You can be a light to give hope to other broken misfits. I am forever thankful for the people God put in my life to share this truth with me. Now, my one mission is to share it with you, and others. This misfit has now found her place and purpose!

EPILOGUE

You have read the stories of fellow misfits and how God changed their lives from horror to healing, destruction to destiny, and pain to purpose. They have laid bare their souls, revealing often embarrassing details and choices in their lives that at one time brought them guilt and shame, while allowing us to see the amazing grace and transforming power of God at work in them. They are now giving back to others who find themselves in difficult and similar situations. I thank them for their honesty, courage, and humility in their desire to encourage and challenge you and honor God's sovereign work and will in their lives. I want to close with a simple outline of how God wants to change your life too:

R – God is the **Ruler** over all, by right of creation – whatever He made, He is the rightful owner, and He makes the rules.

R – Whenever you violate God's rule, you are trying to be the ruler but are actually a **Rebel** against God, committing moral crimes against His sovereign right to rule.

J – All rebellion against God earns **Judgement** or a consequence of separation from a holy God. The wages of sin is death.

J – God sent **Jesus** to rescue us from our well-deserved punishment of eternal separation from God

R – Jesus invites us to **Repent** – to acknowledge our rebellion, confess our sin, and turn to Him for forgiveness and acceptance.

R – The Bible says that to all who **Receive** Jesus as their rescuer and redeemer, God adopts us as His children and gives to us eternal life.

Choose wisely my friend.

God bless.

Chap

Made in the USA
Monee, IL
22 March 2023

29596875R00057